Profiles of rural poverty

This work is a popularised version of *Poverty and landlessness in rural Asia*, published by the ILO in 1977, comprising the results of a series of case studies carried out in eight Asian countries. These were:

Rural poverty and landlessness in Pakistan	S. M. Naseem
Growth and poverty in rural areas of the Indian State of Punjab	Indira Rajaraman
Wages, employment and standard of living of agricultural labourers in Uttar Pradesh	Rohini Nayyar
Poverty and inequality in rural Bihar	Rohini Nayyar
Rural poverty in Tamil Nadu	C. T. Kurien
Poverty and inequality in rural Bangladesh	Azizur Rahman Khan
Rural poverty in Sri Lanka, 1963–73	E. L. H. Lee
Rural poverty in West Malaysia, 1957–70	E. L. H. Lee
Rural poverty in Indonesia with special reference to Java	Ingrid Palmer
Growth and inequality in the rural Philippines	Azizur Rahman Khan
The distribution of income in rural China	Azizur Rahman Khan

Profiles of rural poverty

A popularised version of
Poverty and landlessness in rural Asia,
with additional material on Africa and Latin America

International Labour Office   Geneva

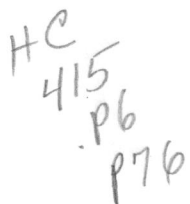

Copyright © International Labour Organisation 1979

Publications of the International Labour Office enjoy copyright under Protocol 2 of the Universal Copyright Convention. Nevertheless, short excerpts from them may be reproduced without authorisation, on condition that the source is indicated. For rights of reproduction or translation, application should be made to the Editorial and Translation Branch, International Labour Office, CH-1211 Geneva 22, Switzerland. The International Labour Office welcomes such applications.

ISBN 92-2-102142-4

First published 1979

The designations employed in ILO publications, which are in conformity with United Nations practice, and the presentation of material therein do not imply the expression of any opinion whatsover on the part of the International Labour Office concerning the legal status of any country or territory or of its authorities, or concerning the delimitation of its frontiers.
The responsibility for opinions expressed in signed articles, studies and other contributions rests solely with their authors, and publication does not constitute an endorsement by the International Labour Office of the opinions expressed in them.

ILO publications can be obtained through major booksellers or ILO local offices in many countries, or direct from ILO Publications, International Labour Office, CH-1211 Geneva 22, Switzerland. A catalogue or list of new publications will be sent free of charge from the above address.

Printed by Imprimeries Populaires, Geneva, Switzerland

PREFACE

For a long time the need has been felt to have certain of the publications issued under the World Employment Programme (WEP) reach a wider audience. Many of the ILO's constituents have expressed the wish that some WEP studies intended in the first place for specialised readers be put in a language accessible to non-specialists. In response to this need it has been decided to produce occasional popularised versions of major WEP research publications. In preparing such versions, however, certain criteria are applied: first, simplifying the technical aspects of the original work cannot involve sacrificing the rigour of the basic argument; secondly, while the evidence supporting various arguments may be summarised or presented in a stylised form, it cannot be overlooked. Sometimes illustrations have been used to point up some of the problems dealt with.

The present booklet, presenting a popularised version of *Poverty and landlessness in rural Asia*, which was published by the ILO in 1977, is a first attempt in this direction. It aims to quantify the level of, and trends in, rural poverty by discussing the major correlates and causes of poverty in some eight Asian countries where the problem is marked. It was also considered useful to add some evidence from other parts of the developing world, especially Africa and Latin America, to provide a comparative perspective. Admittedly the evidence concerning these two continents is not as well documented as in the case of Asia but the few data provided give an indication of the magnitude of the problem there also.

It is our hope that this booklet will serve its intended purpose of reaching a wider audience by arousing the interest, among others, of employers, trade unionists, government officials, rural development workers and students.

Antoinette Béguin,
Chief, Employment and
Development Department

CONTENTS

Preface V

Introduction 1

1. Poverty and landlessness in rural Asia 3
    Advance of rural poverty 4
    Inequality and economic growth 10
    Policies for development 19

2. Profiles of poverty 25
    Bangladesh 26
    Tamil Nadu 29
    Malaysia 33
    China 37

3. Poverty and landlessness in Africa and Latin America 43

Concluding remarks 47
    Lessons and experience 47
    The challenge to the Third World 47

Appendix 49

Conventional signs used in tables
  . = figure not available or category not applicable.
  − = magnitude nil or negligible.

INTRODUCTION

Average income per head in the Third World has grown more rapidly in the past two decades than ever before. Yet development of the type experienced by the majority of those countries has meant, for very large numbers of people, increased impoverishment. This is the main conclusion which has emerged from a series of empirical studies of trends in levels of living in the rural areas of Asia that were reproduced under the title of *Poverty and landlessness in rural Asia*. Ten empirical studies were undertaken in an attempt to determine the trends in absolute and relative incomes of the rural poor in seven Asian countries: Bangladesh, India, Indonesia, Malaysia, Pakistan, the Philippines and Sri Lanka. These countries account for approximately 70 per cent of the rural population of the non-socialist developing world. Since the average income of these seven countries is below that of the rest of the developing market economy countries, it is likely that their share of the poor is even greater.

The most outstanding findings of the study were the worsening distribution of income and the declining real income of the rural poor. Most of the case studies show that the shares of the lower decile groups in aggregate income and consumption have been declining even during periods of relatively rapid agricultural growth. Moreover, evidence from the case studies points to an even stronger conclusion: in each case a significant proportion of low-income households experienced an absolute decline in real income.

These conclusions run contrary to the basic assumptions of the majority of theories and models of economic development which would not lead one to expect that growth of income per head would be associated with the absolute impoverishment of a significant proportion of the population. Alternative explanations were thus sought. A major hypothesis verified by *Poverty and landlessness in rural Asia* is that "the answer to why poverty has increased has more to do with the structure of the economy than its rate of growth". Evidence suggests that unequal distribution of productive assets, especially land, can be identified as the principal factor in the process of poverty generation.

Profiles of rural poverty

The present volume is an attempt to provide a popularised version of these important findings in a language accessible to a wider audience, while remaining faithful to the original work. The booklet begins with a summary outline of the phenomenon of rural poverty in Asia, its extent and causes. Then the general issues are illustrated by the "profiles" of four case studies. Finally an attempt is made to find out to what extent the phenomenon of increasing rural poverty is a general one. Evidence from Africa and Latin America, limited as it may be, suggests that the conclusions reached are by no means unique to Asia, for the mechanisms which generate poverty in Asia are present in greater or lesser degree in much of the rest of the developing world. Certainly there is no evidence that growth as such has succeeded in reducing the incidence of poverty.

The present text, which is an adaptation of the original work, was prepared by Roy Laishley, of the Development Press Services of London. Norman Perryman designed the cover and made the preliminary designs for the charts. Samir Radwan, of the International Labour Office, contributed the part on Africa and Latin America and was responsible for the technical editing of the volume as a whole.

POVERTY AND LANDLESSNESS IN RURAL ASIA

1

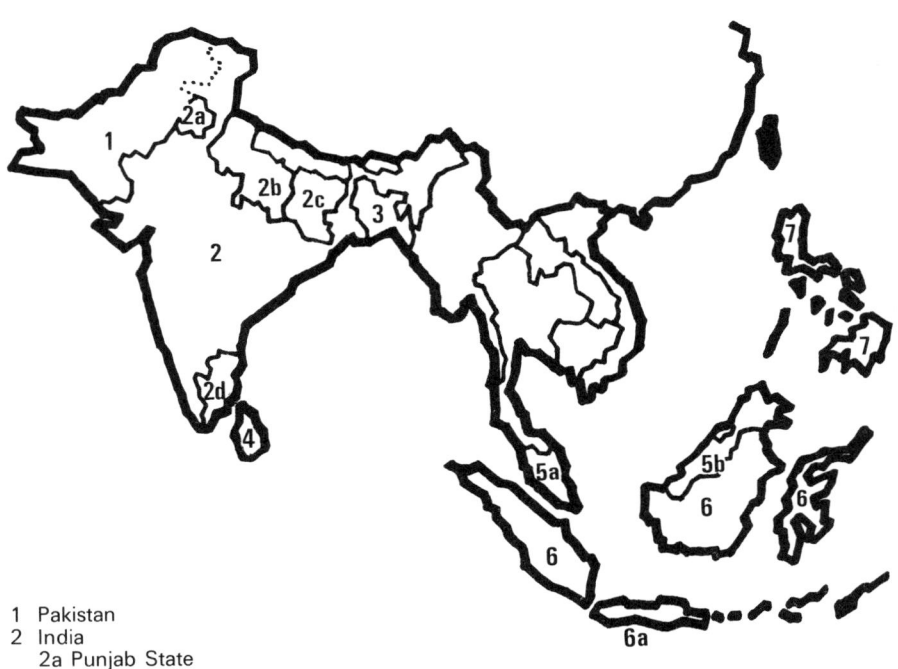

1 Pakistan
2 India
  2a Punjab State
  2b Uttar Pradesh
  2c Bihar
  2d Tamil Nadu
3 Bangladesh
4 Sri Lanka
5 Malaysia
  5a West
  5b East
6 Indonesia
  6a Java
7 Philippines

Profiles of rural poverty

ADVANCE OF RURAL POVERTY: THE EVIDENCE FROM ASIA

Over the past 20 years the number of people in Asia living in poverty has been increasing. In the rural areas of the seven countries with which our studies have been concerned nearly 150 million people were added to the ranks of those without the means to provide for the basic necessities of life. During the same period all but one of these countries experienced a growth in national income of around 2 per cent a year for every member of its population. This is a pattern that holds true for most areas of the developing world.

Why has economic growth in developing countries so often been coupled with increasing poverty? We have examined, in particular, the experience of development in the rural areas of seven south Asian countries in seeking to identify the processes through which this occurs.

Context of poverty

The causes of perpetual poverty and the form that it takes are linked to the nature of the society in which it exists. Charts 1 and 2 describe the basic structure of the seven countries studied.

Most have a very low income per head of the population, with only Malaysia in the middle income range of developing countries. But only in the case of Bangladesh has national income failed to keep pace with the growth in population. Most countries have increased their national income by more than 4 per cent a year, while population has increased at around 2.3 per cent a year on average. This means the amount of income, in theory, available to every person in the region has increased on average by 2 per cent a year.

Chart 3 shows the dominant role agriculture plays in contributing to this income. Manufacturing never accounts for more than 20 per cent of gross national product. More often, industry contributes half this proportion. Agriculture provides most of the remainder and accounts for more than 60 per cent of the labour force in doing so.

But, while national income has been increasing, the benefits of growth have not been distributed evenly.

Charts 4a and 4b show that the poorest 20 per cent of the population do not receive their fair share of national income: on average, only 6 per cent. The richest 20 per cent, on average, enjoy some 48 per cent of national income, and the top 5 per cent 22 per cent. As well as being predominantly agricultural these countries have a high degree of inequality.

Rising poverty

As a result of inequality in the distribution of national income, present rates of economic growth have not been sufficient to raise the standard of living of all the population.

Chart 1. Gross National Product, per head, 1973

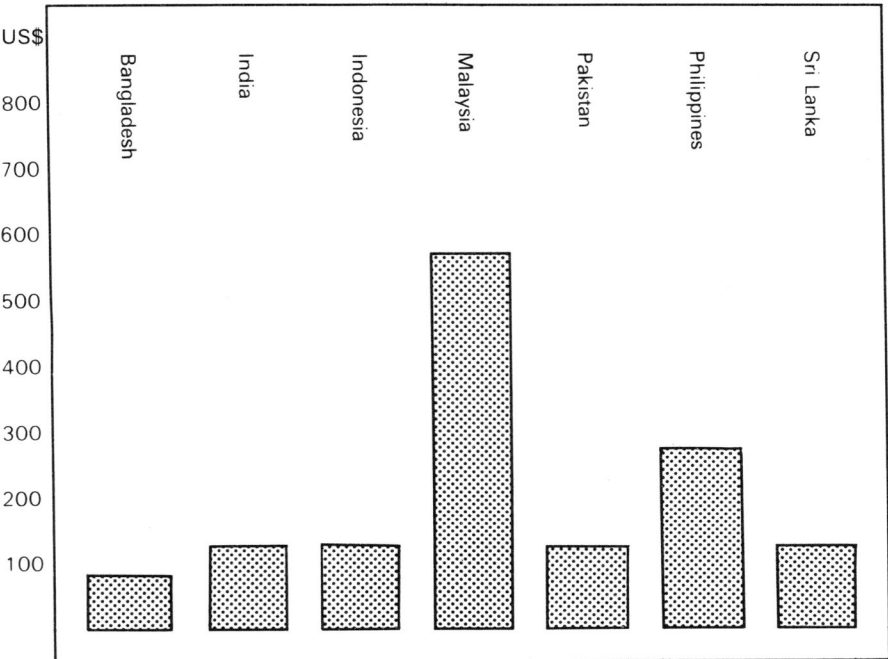

Chart 2. Growth in income and population

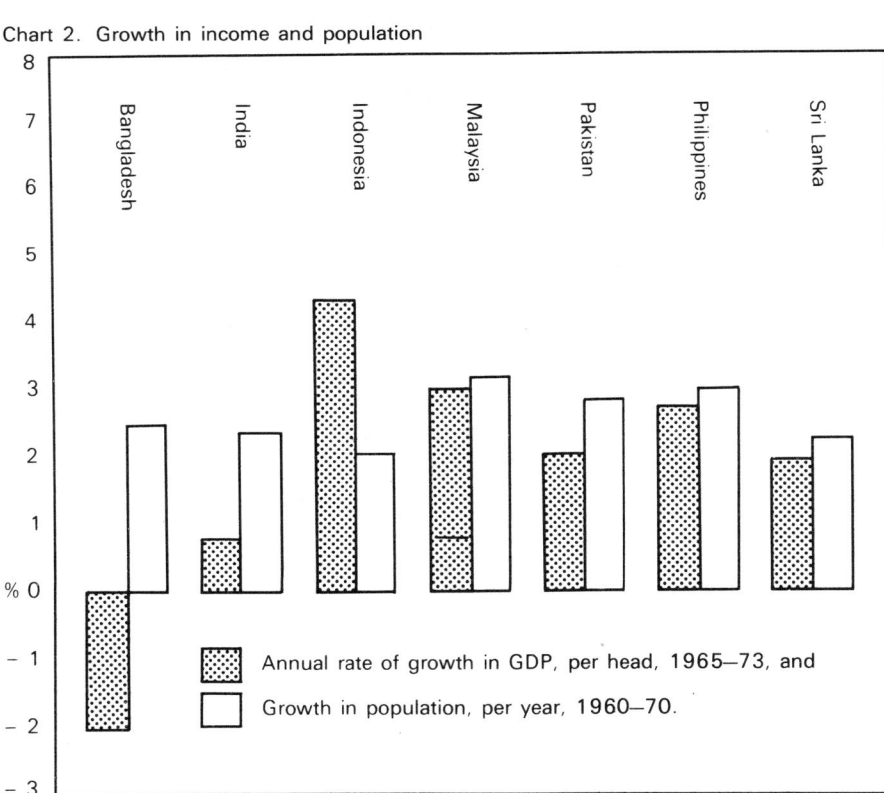

Profiles of rural poverty

Chart 3. The dominance of agriculture

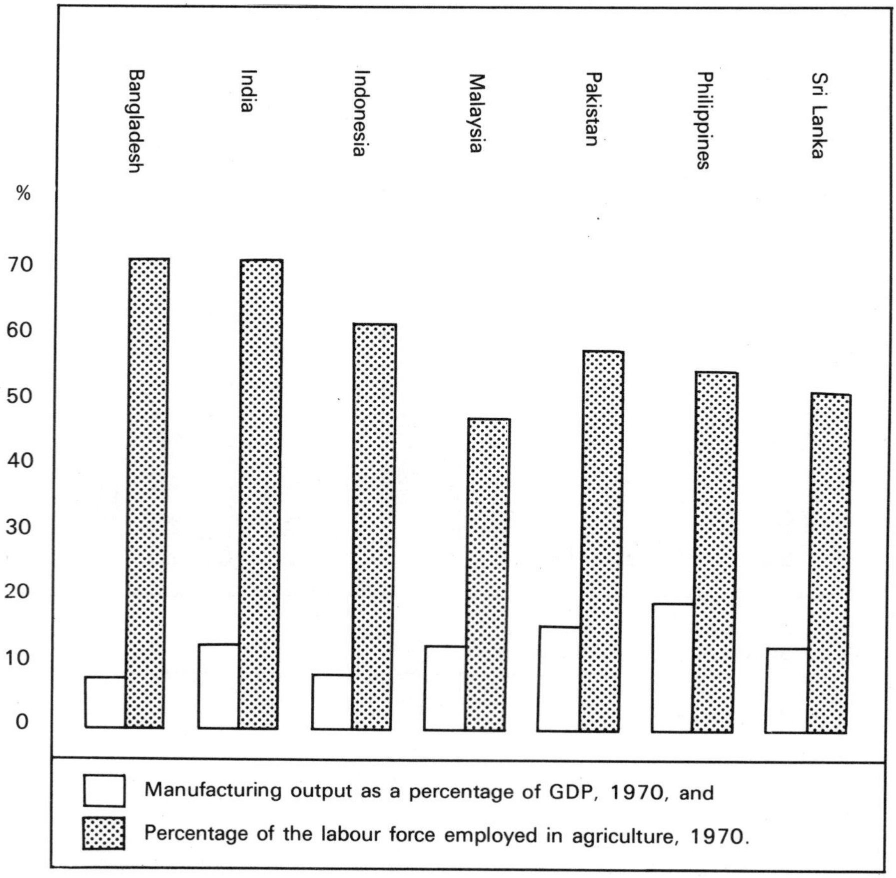

- ☐ Manufacturing output as a percentage of GDP, 1970, and
- ▦ Percentage of the labour force employed in agriculture, 1970.

Note. Gross Domestic Product equals the total value of goods and services produced within a country. Gross National Product is the GDP plus income received from other countries (interest from investments, dividends, etc.) minus similar payments made to other countries. National income is usually GNP with a deduction for the cost of capital assets used up in producing goods and services (i.e. depreciation). Chart 1=GNP and Charts 2 and 3=GDP.

Chart 5 shows the extent of poverty still persisting in the rural areas of eight regions of South Asia. It demonstrates that poverty is not going away. On average, 40 per cent of rural people live below the poverty line; that is, they earn an income less than sufficient to supply their basic needs of food, health, water, housing and education. Behind these stark facts there is a mass of people condemned to hunger, malnutrition and ignorance.

But chart 5 also suggests something far worse. Not only is poverty refusing to go away, it may in some countries be on the increase. In seven of the eight cases studied the proportion of the population living below the

Poverty and landlessness in rural Asia

Chart 4a. The share of rich and poor in national income

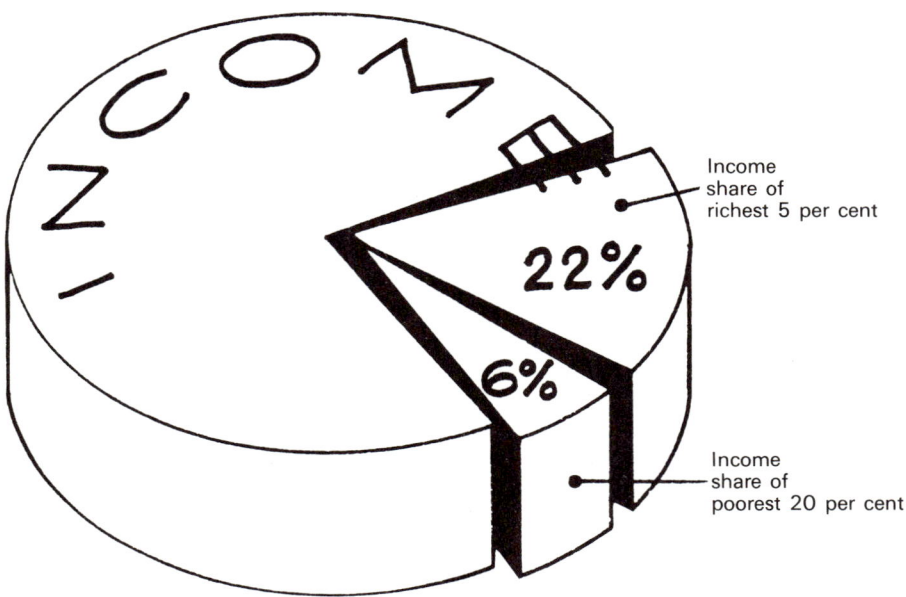

Chart 4b. Percentage of income received by poorest 40 per cent of households

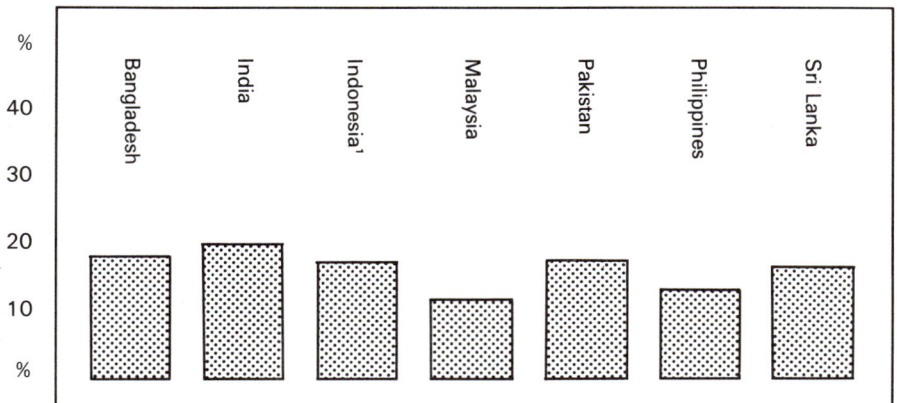

[1] All from *Poverty and landlessness in rural Asia* except for Indonesia, which is based on data from G. Sheehan and M. Hopkins: *Basic needs performance* (Geneva, ILO, 1978, World Employment Programme research working paper, mimeographed; restricted).

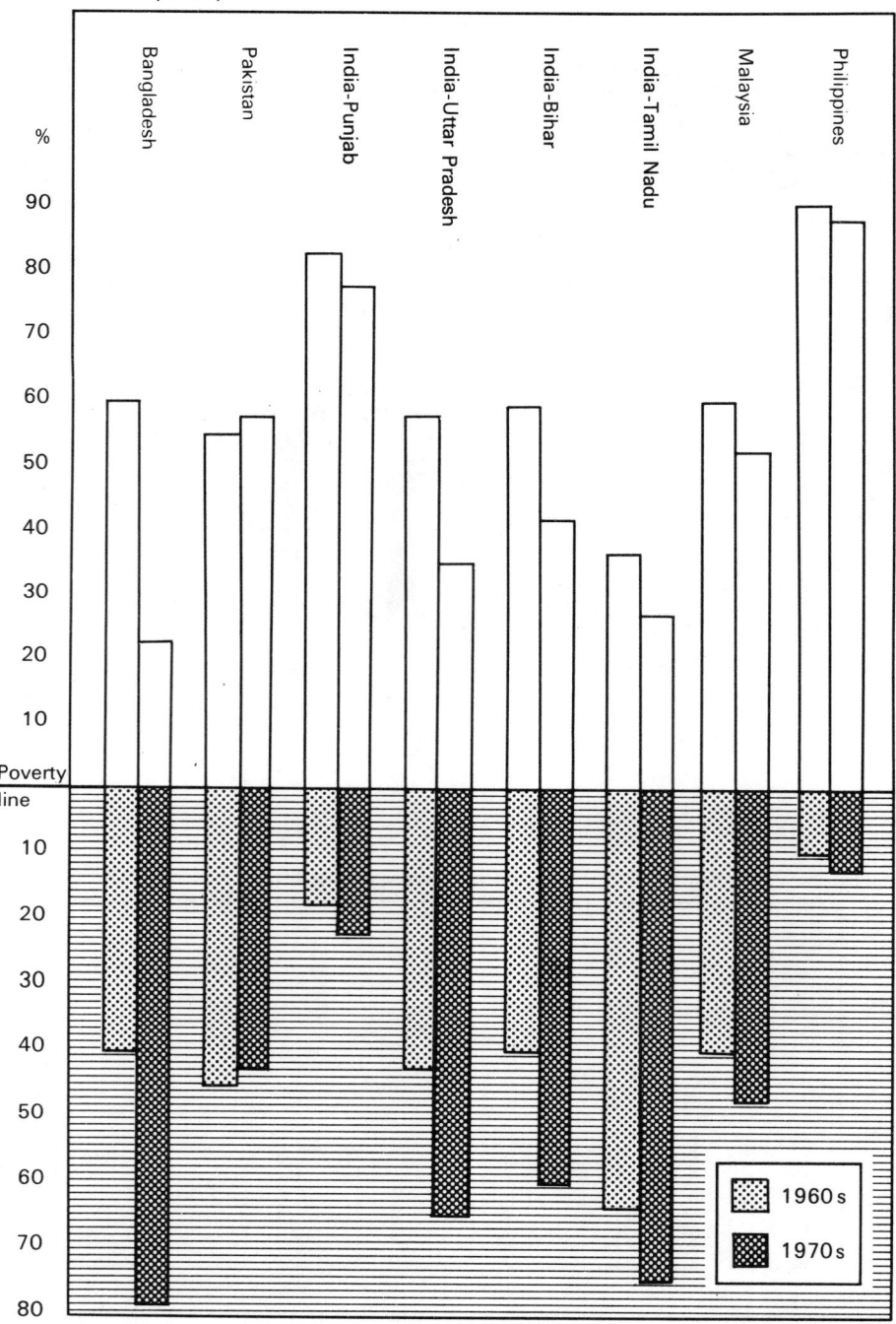

Chart 5. The advance of poverty: percentage of the rural population living above and below the poverty line

Note. See the Appendix for note on this chart.

poverty line was higher in the 1970s than it was in the 1960s. In poor countries like Bangladesh the proportion reaches a frightening 78 per cent; even in the Punjab, where the Green Revolution has raised incomes dramatically, the percentage of the rural population living in poverty has risen.

The increase is not a marginal one; it is not a case of a few more people being slightly less well off. Many people exist on incomes well below the so-called poverty line (for a more detailed discussion of the poverty line see the Appendix).

In Bangladesh between 1963 and 1974 there was a fivefold increase in the proportion of the population considered "extremely poor"; that is, those with a maximum calorie intake only 80 per cent of the calculated minimum. In Sri Lanka, while rice continued to account for 70 per cent of the poorest group's expenditure, its actual per head consumption fell drastically during the 1960s. In the poverty-stricken region of Yogyakarta in Java per head daily consumption of calories fell, between 1960 and 1969, by 16 per cent from a level that was already only two-thirds of the recommended intake for the region.

Who are the poor?

Rural society is highly differentiated. An apparently simple agrarian economy is, in fact, a complex structure of rich landowners, peasants, tenants and labourers. In addition, there are artisans, traders and plantation workers. Poverty strikes unevenly among these groups and the process of economic growth has accentuated the difference in living standards between them. Inevitably it has been the weakest sectors of rural society that have suffered most severely from declining standards of living and worsening poverty.

Everywhere it is the agricultural labourers, the landless and the near-landless who form the core of rural poverty in Asia. In Uttar Pradesh 48 million people were living below the poverty line by the end of the 1960s, nearly all labourers or farmers with tiny plots of land. Ninety-three per cent of agricultural labourers were living below the poverty line. In Tamil Nadu in 1971 56 per cent of cultivators, 85 per cent of "other workers" (mainly artisans) and 87 per cent of agricultural labourers were living below the poverty line that year. In Indonesia, Malaysia, Pakistan and Sri Lanka the pattern of concentration of poverty among the small farmers and the landless is repeated.

In all countries economic growth is failing to make a significant impact in the fight against poverty. The process of growth seems to be forcing more and more of the population into those categories most vulnerable to increasing poverty. This suggests that a process of impoverishment has taken place. Economic prosperity has not simply missed these people; they have been systematically marginalised or proletarianised. Their ability to supply their own basic needs has been gradually but unrelentingly reduced. To

Profiles of rural poverty

explain the increase of poverty in rural Asia we must look at the process of growth itself and at the inequalities in the society in which it takes place.

INEQUALITY AND ECONOMIC GROWTH

Myths

According to the "conventional wisdom" in development literature, as a country increases its income the benefits will "trickle down" to even the poorest members of society. This should happen through the creation of more jobs as the economy expands, better wages as the country earns more and higher prices for farm produce as towns grow. The process can be accelerated and potential bottlenecks removed by the judicious allocation of government incentives and subsidies. It may all take time and the distribution may not be equal, but the incidence of poverty and starvation should be reduced. This has not, in fact, occurred. Poverty refuses to go away. In trying to explain this, many people have argued that population growth has outpaced the rate at which national income and food production have been growing. Chart 2 shows that this is not true for the majority of Asian countries studied. In the past 20 years only Bangladesh has experienced a negative rate of growth per head of the population. Nor can it be argued that insufficient food has been produced.

Chart 6 shows the production of cereals, the staple of everyone's diet. Except in bad years like 1972, production has kept pace with population growth. The margin is a slender one at times, for both income and food, but, taken over-all, rapid population growth by itself cannot explain why, after 20 years of growth, more people are poorer. All else being equal, more than enough has been produced to raise incomes and feed everybody.

But not all else is equal.

The answer to why poverty has increased has more to do with the structure of the economy than its rate of growth. In a society characterised by extreme inequality of income and hence spending power, the very fact of inequality has a number of important consequences. The counterpart to the compression of the income of the poor is the concentration of the economic surplus in the hands of a minority. The way in which this surplus is used in turn largely determines the pace and nature of economic growth. Where the distribution of land is highly unequal the role of large landowners is particularly crucial in determining the wages and incomes of the other members of rural society.

Another reason for the persistence of poverty in rural areas is the pattern of investment in the country as a whole.

The level of investment in developing countries is often extremely low. Where it does occur it favours the towns. There is an "urban bias" in the allocation of investment that deprives the rural areas of much-needed capital.

Poverty and landlessness in rural Asia

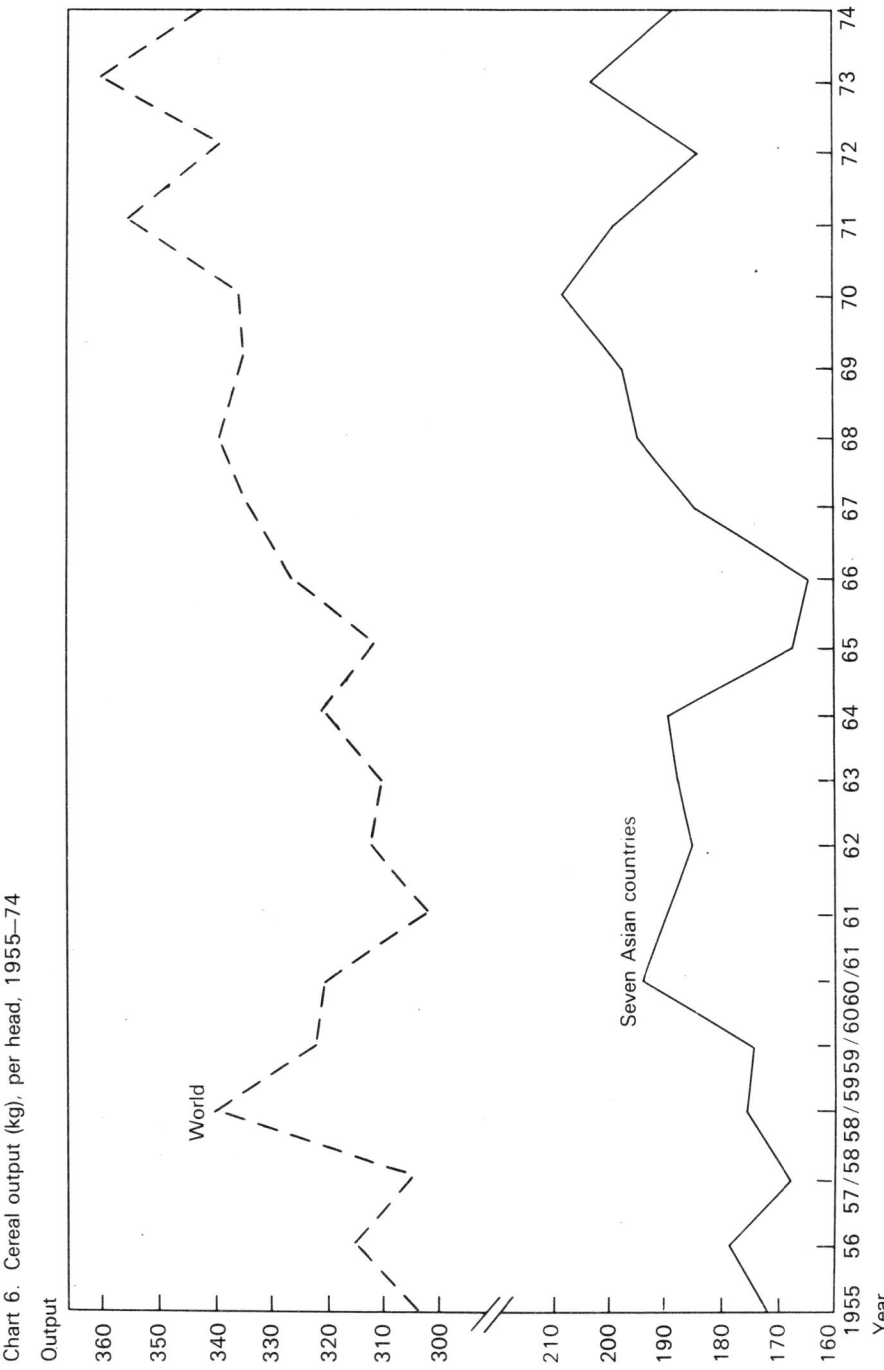

Chart 6. Cereal output (kg), per head, 1955–74

Profiles of rural poverty

Most investment, when it does take place, favours capital-intensive methods of production. While capital generally in developing countries is in short supply, for the rich, with plenty of collateral, money is cheap. The real rate of interest paid by large investors is often negative when inflation is allowed for. This ready availability of capital for a few combines with a dependence on foreign technology to encourage the development of capital-intensive modern industry. The use of labour-saving technology has resulted in a chronically slow rate of job creation in the modern sector. As the case studies demonstrate, this has meant a worsening of unemployment and underemployment.

In the Philippines the proportion of the labour force engaged in manufacturing fell from 13 per cent in 1957 to less than 10 per cent a decade and a half later; at the same time, manufacturing's share of the national product rose from 16 to 20 per cent. A similar decline in manufacturing's share of the labour force is recorded for Bangladesh. In Indonesia the textile industry, which at one time employed almost one-third of all workers in manufacturing, lost half its workers between 1966 and 1971. The handloom and batik sectors lost over 400,000 jobs alone. At the same time that jobs were being lost production increased by 140 per cent.

In rural areas the lack of capital and services creates for the small farmers an overdependence on their most plentiful resource, labour. Lack of access to capital and the improved production techniques it can buy restricts the farmer's ability to raise output by the mere application of a lot more labour time. Large landowners, on the other hand, suffer no such constraints. Their money and influence give them access to both cheap credit and government services. These, in turn, are used to purchase the capital-intensive techniques of production that raise output—and hence the farmer's income—but which fail to generate wider employment.

One group generates income but not jobs, while the small farmer, constrained in his access to land and capital, finds a ceiling imposed on his ability to increase his income. As a result his demand for hired labour is reduced. In both cases it is the landless wage earner who is ultimately squeezed. In addition, the concentration of land among a few major landowners allows them sufficient cohesion to assert a dominant control over the returns to labour. Through the wages they pay their labourers and the rents they demand from their tenants, the rich directly control the income of the poor.

In theory, government policy can ease this problem by encouraging a reorientation of investment on the one hand and by helping to remove the constraints on the small farmer on the other. But the consequences of inequality make themselves felt here as well. Inequality in the possession of land reproduces itself in the distribution system. Hence the maldistribution in incomes and productive assets is then reinforced by a maldistribution of those socially provided goods and services that can supplement income.

The Green Revolution

Our case studies demonstrate just how growth in the rural economy has failed to make any significant impact on poverty. The most dramatic example of this problem has been the Green Revolution.

The most popularly advocated solution to rural poverty is to raise food production as quickly and as dramatically as possible. Starvation, hunger and malnutrition would, it is argued, disappear with the introduction of new high-yielding varieties of wheat, rice and other cereals. The Green Revolution is a mix of these "wonder seeds", coupled with increased and improved irrigation, fertilisers and improved production techniques, such as mechanisation.

In a technological sense most of the Green Revolution package is scale-neutral—it is as efficient on small farms as on large ones; the major exception, in some cases, is the use of tractors. But in a situation of structural inequality the impact of the Green Revolution has been far from neutral. Output has increased in the areas where the programmes have been applied, average incomes have even risen, but the Green Revolution has failed to promote a wider development. Instead, in many cases, it has merely sustained the structure of inequality at the cost of increasing poverty.

In the rich farmlands of India's Punjab the new techniques of the Green Revolution have brought a vast increase in the production of wheat. Real income per head (that is, allowing for inflation) rose by 26 per cent during the 1960s; two-and-a-half times as fast as in India as a whole. Despite this the proportion of the rural population living below the poverty line increased from 18 per cent in 1960 to 23 per cent ten years later. Similar situations exist in other regions.

Everywhere the gains from the Green Revolution have depended on the command of resources—land, capital and influence. The structure of inequality determines the pattern this has taken. Large landowners, with the necessary capital, are the ones who can most easily apply the new techniques; rich farmers are the ones with the influence to secure cheap credit or the usually scarce quantities of fertiliser. The inequality in the distribution of agricultural services between farmers applies to geographical regions as well. It is the richer, more accessible regions that have acquired the bulk of benefits flowing from the Green Revolution.

In some areas the Green Revolution has contributed directly to a worsening of inequality by increasing the concentration of operated land. Where this has occurred it has primarily been because of a reduction in tenancies as the rising returns to agricultural production encourage landowners to farm the land themselves. This is particularly marked where the adoption of tractors has facilitated the cultivation of larger farming units.

In Pakistan 42 per cent of additionally farmed land by tractor-owning farmers came from old rented lands, 36 per cent from newly acquired land and only 22 per cent from land that had not previously been cultivated.

Profiles of rural poverty

With 80 per cent of new land coming from other farmers this means land concentration is getting worse and landlessness increasing.

In Bangladesh distress sales of land have been worsened by the inflationary effects of growth in a situation where access to income-earning opportunities has been constrained.

Lack of demand for labour

The sale of land by small farmers also points to the lack of alternative income-earning opportunities in the form of wage labour. Over-all, the new agricultural techniques should employ more people. Evidence from Uttar Pradesh suggests that the increased use of fertiliser and irrigation and more careful sowing and harvesting can result in a 58 per cent increase in the amount of labour time needed on every crop. For rice it has been generally calculated that pre-harvest tasks can involve a 33 per cent increase in demand for labour. However, the manner in which the Green Revolution has been implemented means that, more often than not, it has reduced labour demand, not raised it.

Generally, the Green Revolution investment has followed its urban counterpart in being capital intensive and geared to a labour-saving process of technical innovation. The use of tractors is a prime example. In Pakistan it has been calculated that the introduction of each tractor leads to the loss of five jobs, particularly in ploughing and soil-preparation tasks. With some 40,000 tractors in use this means that 200,000 jobs have disappeared. Pakistan is a wheat-growing area, but the labour-displacing nature of much of the Green Revolution is equally true for rice as well. In Indonesia harvesting innovations alone have led to a fall of 104 man-days per hectare where it has been applied. Often such innovations fall on one particular sector of the rural labour force. In Indonesia rice mills are now quickly replacing the traditional hand-pounding of rice. It has been calculated that this will reduce the required workforce for this task from nearly 400,000 full-time workers to a mere 33,000 if bulk facilities are used and if small village mills are installed still by half. This could mean a loss of 125 million work days for the women who originally hand-pounded rice. This means a loss in earnings to them of some US$55 million.

Over-all, the Green Revolution has failed to raise significantly the demand for wage labour. Often labour has been displaced and where the demand has been raised it has been absorbed by under-utilised family time rather than with hired labour.

Increase in landlessness

Such a pattern of growth can operate on an already acutely unequal distribution of productive assets to actually increase poverty. Among cultivators the distribution of land is very unequal, despite frequent land-reform legislation. In India often more than half of all land is owned by the top

Poverty and landlessness in rural Asia

10 per cent of landowners, while the majority of farmers must be content with less than 1 acre. Chart 7 shows that, in the other countries as well, a large percentage of farms fall into the smallest size group.

In Pakistan, in 1960, the 50 per cent of farmers with the smallest holdings accounted for only 10 per cent of the cultivated area, while the top 8 per cent of farms accounted for 42 per cent of all land. In the Philippines, at the same time, the top 0.2 per cent of farms accounted for over 12 per cent of the land. In Sri Lanka the smallest 65 per cent of farmers possessed only 20 per cent of cultivated land in 1970.

At the same time only 50 per cent of rural households are in direct possession of land. The remainder are dependent on wage labour, trade or government service. Because of the small size of their farms many cultivating families supplement their income by such other activities.

While a few rich farmers are benefiting from economic growth, an increasing proportion of farmers have been compelled to supplement their income by wage labour. Smaller holdings, lack of capital and population increase combine to intensify the labour input into cultivation. Without adequate use of other factors such as water and fertilisers—artificial or natural—the pressure for more food creates increasing over-exploitation of the soil, declining productivity and hence falling incomes and food intake. Many farmers accumulate debts, mortgaging their land in order to gain more money. To buy food and pay back debts many are forced to sell their land.

Many small farmers are becoming more and more dependent on wage labour. As a result, agricultural labourers represent a large and increasing section of rural society. The growth in their numbers has far outpaced the average growth of the rural population. Chart 8 shows their rise in India during the 1970s.

In the rural Punjab of India small farmers and the landless account for 49 per cent of households; in Tamil Nadu the figure is closer to 60 per cent. In Java nearly 75 per cent of rural households had less than 0.5 hectare of land, the minimum considered necessary by local farmers to meet their own version of the "poverty line". Since the beginning of the century some 30 million people have been added to the category of landless in Java alone. In Pakistan, between 1951 and 1961, the number of landless labourers increased by 350 per cent from 0.14 million to 0.61 million.

In this situation the failure of economic growth to secure a faster rate of job creation becomes crucial. With numbers increasing at the same time that employment is often falling, the wages of agricultural labourers have declined in many regions.

Chart 9 shows that, at the very least, the real wages of agricultural labourers (adjusting them for inflation) fluctuate wildly from year to year. Some years they are relatively high, more often they are low. But, in three out of the five examples, wages failed to rise at all, or even fell dramatically. As these wages relate to daily rates the decline in the number of days worked throughout the year means that the real income of an increasingly

Profiles of rural poverty

Chart 7. Percentage of farming households with less than 1 acre of land

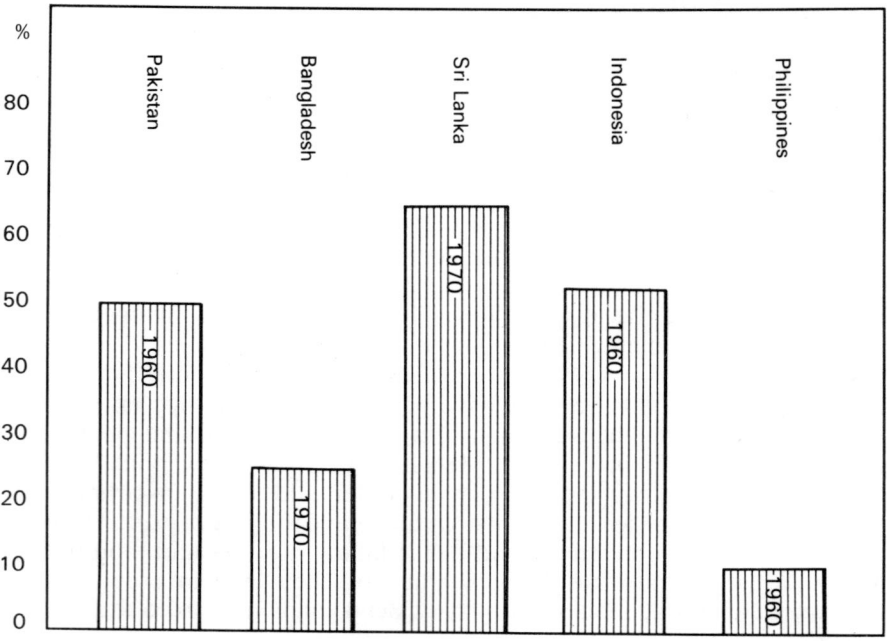

Chart 8. The rising number of landless in India: agricultural labourers as a percentage of the rural labour force, 1960 and 1970

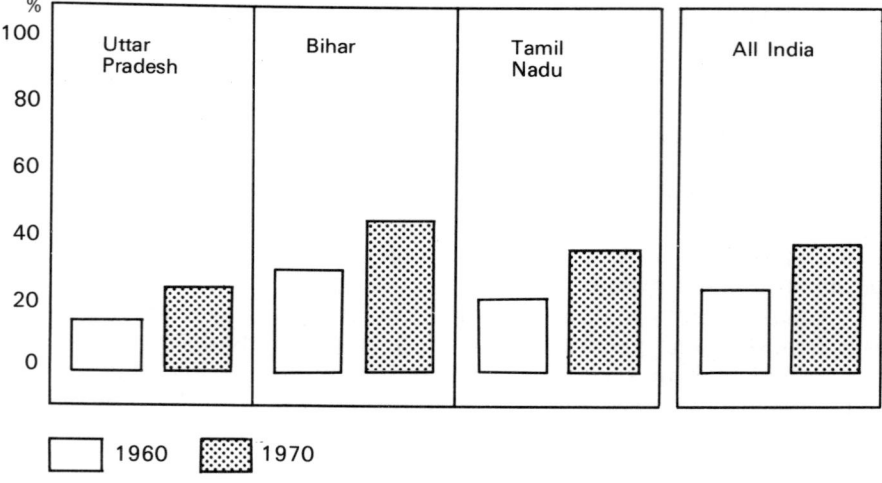

Poverty and landlessness in rural Asia

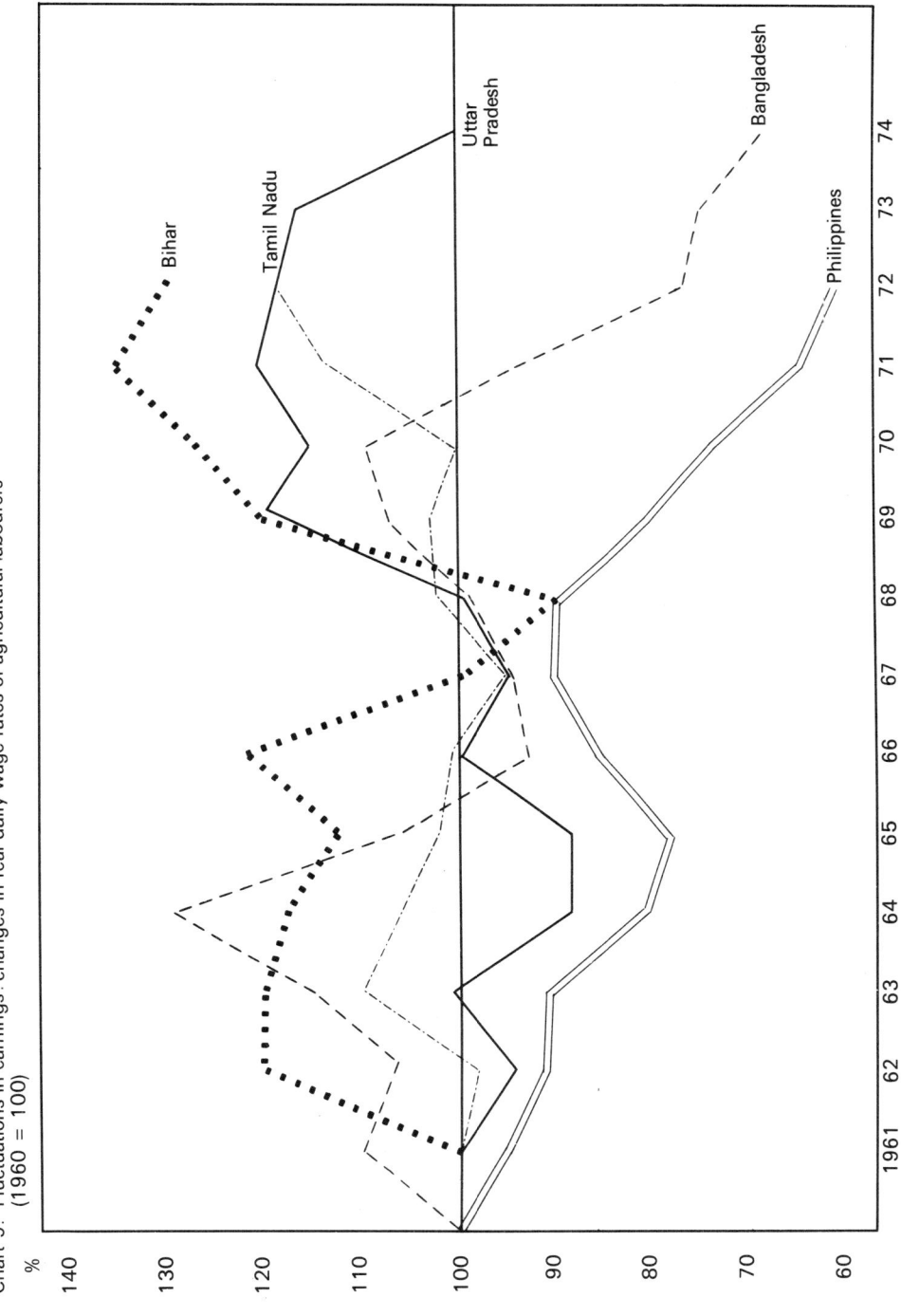

Chart 9. Fluctuations in earnings: changes in real daily wage rates of agricultural labourers (1960 = 100)

Profiles of rural poverty

large section of rural society is falling sharply from its already unacceptably low levels.

In India's Uttar Pradesh the number of agricultural labourers increased from 3.2 million in 1961 to 5.4 million a decade later; a rise of 6.8 per cent per annum compared with the state's average population increase of only 2 per cent. Population growth, migration and the decline in the number of small and tenant farmers all played their part. The result was a stagnation in both the number of days worked and in real daily wage rates. With a doubling in the cost of the minimum income estimated necessary to keep a family above the poverty line, the number of poor rose from 27 million to 48 million.

Landlessness in an agrarian society represents an alienation from the principal source of income generation: land. The rise in landlessness means that fewer and fewer people in rural Asia can directly control their supply of food and income. In such a category we may also include the small farmer with insufficient land to feed his family and, in many cases, the tenant farmer who is deprived of any security over either his farm or his crops. The precariousness of such an agrarian structure becomes manifest when employment fails to increase or incomes fail to keep pace with inflation.

Impact of more people

It is in this context that population growth makes its impact on the standard of living of certain groups in rural areas. Population growth in Asia averages between 2 and 3 per cent a year. This high, but not necessarily excessive, rate can have a devastating impact when land is not available to the majority of the people, job creation is slow and family incomes are stagnant.

Six mouths to feed where there had been five before is important because the chance to earn more money or to grow more food is not there for large numbers of the rural population. Fast population growth, of itself, does not explain poverty.

Not by growth alone

Where economic growth has occurred in the rural areas it has been limited to those with sufficient command of resources, and often has been labour-displacing in its effect.

Inequality in access to land and capital has combined with the capital-intensive character of economic growth to bring enormous profits to a few and increasing poverty to the majority.

Small farmers have found their incomes stagnant as access to land and capital has become more difficult. The increasing number of landless labourers have found their income declining as underemployment worsens. Income inequality has increased (see chart 10) and in many cases land

Poverty and landlessness in rural Asia

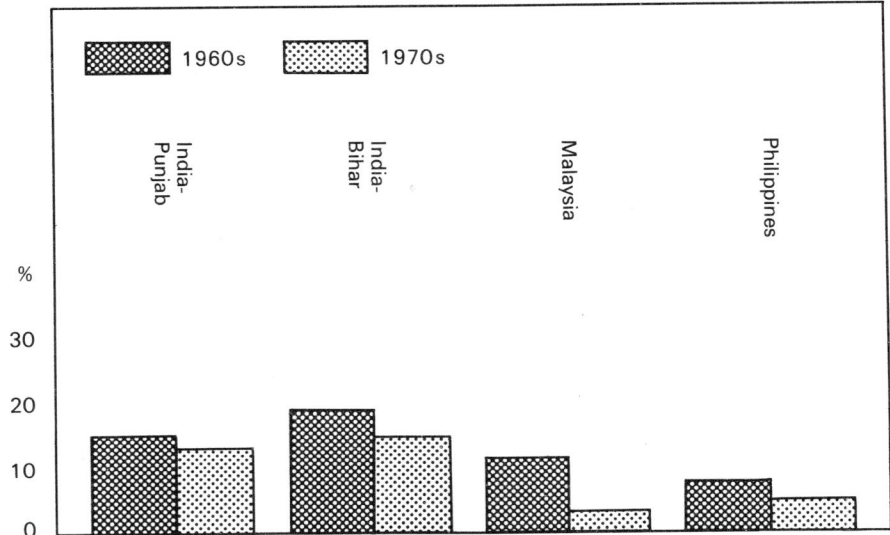

Chart 10. The growth of inequality: shares of the poorest 20 per cent in rural income

concentration as well. And with a dramatic rise in the incomes of the rich has come a general price inflation that proved catastrophic to the stagnant incomes of small farmers and rural labourers alike. The consequence has been an advancing poverty line in the midst of apparent plenty.

POLICIES FOR DEVELOPMENT

Growth plus

The key to greater prosperity for the poor is a combination of greater equality and faster growth. The task is a formidable one.

Work done by the ILO for the 1976 World Employment Conference suggested that, in order to meet the basic needs of all the population–in food, housing, sanitation and education–within one generation, without any redistribution of productive assets, it would be necessary to double the rate of economic growth achieved in recent years by most Asian countries. Such a target would seem beyond most countries' present capabilities.

A feasible alternative–a combination of growth and a redistribution of income–was suggested by the ILO. With more assets in the hands of the poor, growth would have to average something like 6 per cent a year in order that basic needs–in theory–can be met. This still represents a formidable task, particularly as it assumes at least a doubling in the income share of the poorest section of the population.

Profiles of rural poverty

Such an increase in their share of rural income is unlikely to be secured by the poor through a greater share in the increments of growth alone. The poor would have to increase vastly their share of new services, new jobs and raise substantially their rates of pay. In a society riven by inequality the gains from new growth tend to flow in quite the opposite way. Even if governments ensured that all new projects were aimed specifically at benefiting the poor they could not help but benefit the rich as well. New roads help rich and poor alike. Worse, increases in wage rates for labourers could raise food prices, with a consequent adverse effect on demand and thereby producing a "kickback" effect on agricultural employment.

A simple redistribution of income, even if it were passionately pursued, would be a long-winded procedure and very difficult to control. There is no guarantee that it could succeed and every reason to believe that there would be sufficient countervailing pressures to ensure that it would not meet its objective. Thus, a substantial portion of the population would continue to live well below the poverty line.

What is required is an initial redistribution of productive assets. A redistribution of the wealth that enables people to control their incomes and ensure that they can at least provide a minimum standard of living for their family. In agricultural countries this implies above all the need for land reform.

Redistribution of land

In land-scarce Asia a reduction in the inequality of landownership through a redistribution of land to landless workers, tenants and small farmers would be the most direct and effective way to reduce the most acute forms of poverty. Land reform is the key to breaking the deadly link between economic growth and the perpetuation of poverty. Joined to this must be a more careful–and more equal–distribution of new and vital services and resources for agriculture.

Land reform

Land reform has been proclaimed the key to rural development in many countries for many years. But for a number of reasons it has failed in its task.

Too many exemptions

Loopholes in much of the legislation allows many landowners to wriggle out of the law to hand over land. In Pakistan the 1959 Act allowed landlords to transfer land to their sons before their land was taken away. Orchards and livestock farms were exempt. In Sri Lanka the 1972 Land Reform Act made exempt land held by public companies.

Difficult to enforce

Even where legislation covers all cases, making sure landlords do hand over excess land is extremely difficult. Disguised sub-letting, fragmented holdings and the false declaration of rent income give the rich ample opportunity to evade the law.

Land ceilings too high

The main feature of land-reform legislation has been a maximum ceiling on individual holdings. In many cases this has been too high. In the 1959 Pakistan Act the ceiling was 500 acres of irrigated or 1,000 acres of non-irrigated land. That the 1972 Land Reform Act reduced these ceilings to 150 and 300 acres respectively indicates the laxity of earlier legislation. Even then it has been estimated that no more than 16 per cent of tenants under present conditions could possibly benefit. In Sri Lanka, too, the 25-acre ceiling in the 1972 legislation is very high, when the average size of holdings in 1970 was only 1.52 acres.

Landless ignored

Most of the present legislations distribute land only to existing tenants or other farmers. This ignores the 40 per cent of the rural population who are landless.

Much of the impressive-sounding legislation has had a minimal impact on land redistribution. Over-all, very few families have benefited. In Pakistan, for instance, probably 250,000 farm families, or only 5 per cent of the total number of farmers, have benefited. But land reform can be effective. In South Korea, for instance, more pervasive legislation has succeeded in significantly redistributing land, and in China the same was achieved through different methods.

Land reform will have a greater impact if it distributes land to the landless as well as tenants and involves directly the rural people.

While the case for land reform can be made solely on the grounds of equity, it is also likely to increase economic growth. Small farms, typically, have a higher output per acre and employ more labour per acre than larger farms. This is because they use more labour-intensive techniques and farm their land more intensively.

Other measures

It would be wrong to think of land reform as a panacea for all times and conditions. In fact, experience shows that it is a necessary but by no means a sufficient condition for egalitarian development, and it should be complimented by other measures. Examples follow.

Distributional and regional policies

Of prime importance is access to the complex of agricultural extension services—credit, seeds, water, fertilisers and marketing facilities—and to regional infrastructure such as roads and transport. Strategic to the equal distribution of these is the role of the government. It alone can overcome the accident of location—rich soils, proximity to towns—and the more deliberate exploitation of wealth, influence and power that ensures a chronic inequality in the distribution of these essential services.

This means reconsidering regional policies so that they positively favour the poorer regions. This problem has not been eradicated in China, where a fourfold difference in income between the richest commune and the poorest provides one of the greatest sources of inequality in the rural areas.

A move away from large-scale projects towards small-scale development is also important. Action should be aimed at the needs of the weaker sectors. Irrigation networks designed to feed small farm units, credit facilities restricted to farms of certain size or income would help to provide a more equal distribution of a nation's resources. New schemes should try to ensure that the labour input is maximised to the extent compatible with maintaining efficiency. All this should be carried out within a general re-orientation of public expenditure towards agricultural and regional policies.

Co-operatives [1]

In many cases the more active extension of central government into the rural areas will be facilitated by the organisation of farmers into co-operatives. In land-scarce areas this is particularly important, but elsewhere co-operatives will permit more rational production, more equal access to extension facilities and a saving of costs, particularly in marketing.

But there are dangers, as existing schemes demonstrate. Governments will have to take rural development schemes more seriously. The terms of trade for agricultural products (that is, movements in the price of wheat, for example, relative to the movement in the price of manufactured goods) have consistently worsened in many areas. In some cases this has been a deliberate effect of government policy: an extraction of economic surplus from the rural areas to finance the industrial development in the towns.

The other danger is that the advantages of co-operatives can be taken over by the larger farmers. Attempts to counter this can be frustrated in an infinite number of ways. Examples of the Comilla projects in Bangladesh and Pakistan illustrate the point. [2]

A more decentralised system, heavily dependent on the participation of all local people in the formulation as well as the running of the new programme, seems to be a necessary part of any new approach. For this, rural-based organisations and co-operatives need to be encouraged.

Wage labour

The principle of co-operation applies not just to farmers but to wage labourers as well. Export crops may have an adverse effect on food production and income distribution, but the industrial-like organisation of the rural plantation has facilitated the organisation of labour. In countries like Malaysia (rubber) and India (tea) plantation workers have been notable for their ability, through their unions, to maintain wage levels. In Malaysia estate wages increased by almost 40 per cent, a phenomenal increase when compared with normal farm wage rates.

The notoriously difficult task of organising farm workers into effective unions would seem essential if guarantees against continuing poverty are to be attained. Again, the organisation and structure must be rural-based and depend upon the active participation of labouring families.

Frequently revised and more conscientiously applied, minimum wage legislation (coupled with conditions of work legislation) are necessary parts of any new strategy to reduce poverty. But they are impotent tools without effective unionisation; and unionisation is dependent on more fundamental change.

Conclusion

The eradication of poverty from where it is most extensive–the rural areas–cannot be brought about by a single solution. It requires a complex series of interlocking policies. Economic growth must continue and if possible at a faster pace; but more of it must take place in the countryside. The reorientation of public investment towards the rural areas and to agriculture is vital if this new pattern of growth is to occur. With it must come a greater precision in creating new resources geared to the small farmer, the agricultural labourer and to other vulnerable groups in the rural population. The objective of such policies must be, with due awareness of their possible "spin-off" effects, to raise substantially the income-earning power of the mass of the rural poor.

For such a combination of policies to succeed two prior conditions must be achieved. One is a substantial redistribution of land. No programme can hope to guarantee the mass of rural people economic security until the majority have access to the principal source of wealth in the countryside-land. Anything less ensures a greater reward to the more fortunate–a luxury the poor cannot afford if all are to achieve their basic needs within the next 20 years.

Finally, a more effective development policy by central government is dependent upon the more active participation of the mass of the rural people in the political and decision-making process. The structure of inequality restricts the ability of governments to carry out a policy in contradiction to the logic suggested by the concentration of economic power in relatively few hands. Such a structure favours an exclusive, self-generating growth based on capital-intensive means of production.

Profiles of rural poverty

It follows that only the active involvement of rural people in the construction of a new growth strategy can hope to ensure that all the people benefit. This means involving people in the formulation and execution of land-reform programmes, the establishment of rural co-operatives and in building up labour organisations.

Notes

[1] The discussion in this section draws on other ILO research. C.f. D. Ghai, A. R. Khan, E. Lee and S. Radwan (eds.): *Agrarian systems and rural development* (Macmillan, 1979).

[2] A. R. Khan: "The Comilla Model and the Integrated Rural Development Programme of Bangladesh", ibid.

PROFILES OF POVERTY   2

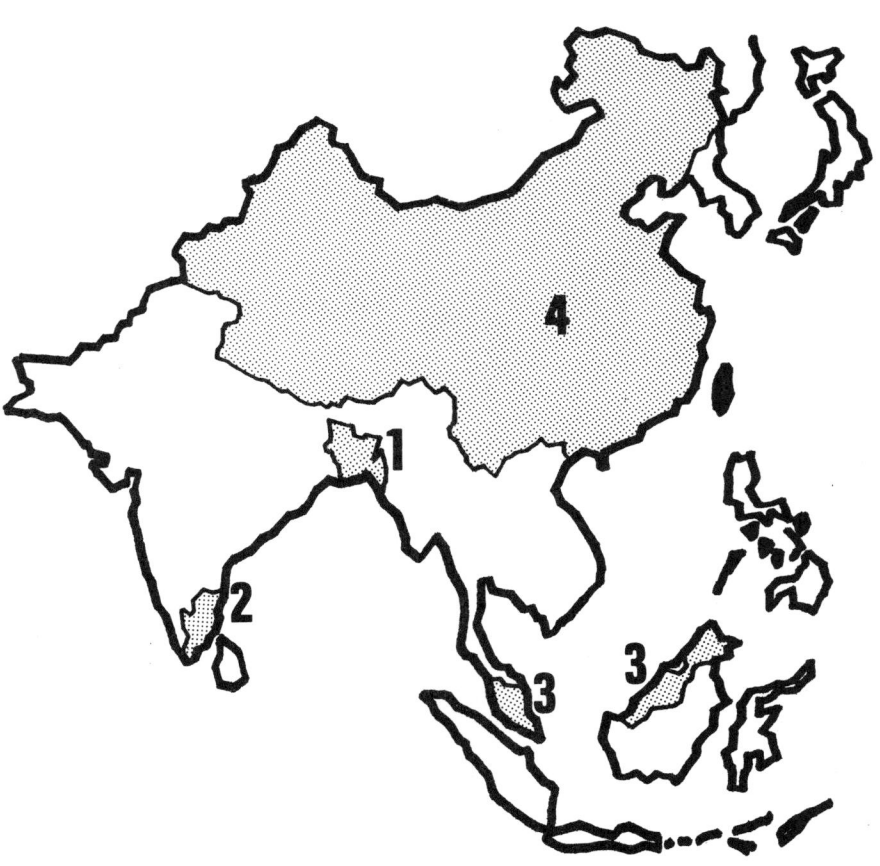

1 Bangladesh
2 Tamil Nadu
3 Malaysia
4 China

Profiles of rural poverty

BANGLADESH: POVERTY WITHOUT GROWTH

Bangladesh is a small country; little more than the great delta of the Ganges and Brahmaputra rivers. Yet, crowded into its 143,000 square kilometers, is a population of 79 million, making it the eighth most populated country in the world. Only four countries (China, India, Indonesia and the USSR) have a larger rural population and only three (China, India and Indonesia) have more people directly dependent on agriculture for a living.

Rice is the–not so secure–mainstay of the economy; the other major crop is jute. For most of the year jute acreage is small (abour 7 per cent), but in the mid-monsoon season this rises to nearly 25 per cent of the total cultivated acreage. Jute–raw or manufactured–accounts for 90 per cent of Bangladesh's exports.

With so many people and so little land, the land : man ratio is very low, only 0.4 acre of land for every member of agricultural households. The economy is precarious and a low growth rate in agricultural production has been made worse by the devastation of floods and hurricanes. Bangladesh's population is growing at around 2.6 per cent per annum, which is about the average rate for the region. But investment in rural areas has been low and with food production increasing at only 2 per cent per annum the number of people is outpacing the food supply.

To an already precarious and poverty-stricken economy, a high degree of inequality has added an unprecedented concentration of extreme poverty in rural Bangladesh today.

Advance of poverty

The availability of information for the years 1963-64 and for 1973-74 allows us to assess the impact of poverty during the late 1960s and early 1970s.

Table 1 shows the proportion of the rural population living in poverty. The concept of "absolute poverty" used in the table indicates an income calculated to be sufficient to provide a family with 90 per cent of its calorie needs–provided they are in a position to spend the money efficiently. The concept of "extreme poverty" means an income that would supply only 80 per cent of those calories. If the more official poverty lines for Bangladesh are taken, 96 per cent of rural households in 1963-64 would have been below that line.

As it was, over half the rural households in that period were absolutely poor and about 10 per cent extremely poor. This is an optimistic figure. While income-based poverty lines may underestimate the degree of consumption from home-grown produce, the calorie requirements assumed here, for people engaged in hard, exacting work, under the most trying of conditions, are certainly too low. The lack of sufficient food is, therefore,

Profiles of poverty

Table 1. The advance of poverty
(Percentage of the total rural population)

Year	Absolutely poor		Extremely poor	
	Households	Population	Households	Population
1963-64	51.7	40.2	9.8	5.2
1973-74	86.7	78.5	54.1	42.1

even greater. This is true for protein intake as well which, for the two groups, appears to be only 78 and 70 per cent of the United Nations recommended level. It can be safely assumed that those called "absolutely poor" are severely undernourished and those called "extremely poor" are in a state of acute malnutrition for most of the year.

Yet, incredibly, the number of people living in poverty has increased, with many slipping even further below the level of extreme poverty. In 1973-74 87 per cent of all rural households were absolutely poor and 54 per cent of them extremely poor. The rise in the number of the really desperately poor has been phenomenal and a great number of these will be living on incomes far below that which would provide them with even 80 per cent of their food requirements. Other basic needs are even more limited. There is virtually a complete absence of public health services in rural Bangladesh. Expenditure by labouring households on health and education is almost non-existent. Nearly 90 per cent of labourers are illiterate, compared with an average of 73 per cent for the rural population (aged above 10) as a whole.

Context of poverty

Two basic facts account for this vast increase in poverty. One is a structural shift in the income-earning opportunities of the rural population, which has depressed incomes; the other is a crippling rise in the price of rice, partly the result of poor production and shortages. The two together have obliterated the purchasing power of the vast majority of the rural population.

Dependence on rice

The demand for rice has resulted in a steady rise in the price of this basic foodstuff. As poorer households spend a far greater proportion of their income on food than do those in the higher-income brackets (70–80 per cent compared with 40 per cent or less) their cost of living has gone up that much more. Between 1964 and 1974 high-income groups experienced a 388 per cent increase in their cost of living; for the low-income groups the cost of living rose by 465 per cent!

A rigid agricultural system ties people to rice. Wheat, boosted by food aid, is the only substitute, but little of it gets to the rural areas. In 1963-64 wheat accounted for only 6.6 per cent of the consumption of cereals, but its share rose to 12.6 per cent in 1973-74. This increase, however, was concentrated in urban areas where statutory rationing of imported wheat was introduced. In the rural areas the free market for wheat was insignificant and the small quantities distributed through a "modified rationing" scheme probably never accounted for more than 5 per cent of total cereal consumption in those areas.

Dependence on wages

Even in the mid-1960s nearly a sixth of the agriculturally active population depended entirely on wages as a source of income. For a quarter of the population wages were a major source. This dependence has been increasing.

Table 2 shows the growing number of landless in rural Bangladesh. The numbers of labourers increased by 5.4 per cent per annum during these years, compared with an average population growth of 2.6 per cent. At the same time the average number of days worked by labourers declined. The shift from jute to rice, because of the higher price of the latter, worsened this. The labour input for jute can be nearly double that needed for rice.

Increasing landlessness is in part explained by distress sales of land by small farmers. Their incomes squeezed between poor productivity (resulting from a lack of capital) and rising inflation, 60 per cent of farmers in the smallest land-holding category sold some of their land in 1972-73, compared with only 4 per cent among large farmers. The total acreage cultivated by tenants declined and the distribution of land among the remaining landowners became less equal, as an increasing proportion joined the category of small or "below subsistence" cultivators.

The reduction in the self-sufficiency of so many farmers threw them on to an already crowded labour market, itself the result of population growth combined with low levels of rural investment. The urban areas did not provide an alternative source of income for the majority. The manufacturing sector's share in total employment declined from 5.8 per cent in 1963-64 to 5.4 per cent in 1967-68 and has probably declined even further.

The consequence has been a decline in the real wage rate for agricultural labourers (see chart 9). In 1964 labourers were getting 2.66 takas a day; by 1974, allowing for the rate of inflation, the equivalent pay was only 1.42 takas a day. Declining real wages, coupled with fewer days worked throughout the year, ate into the purchasing power of labourers' incomes, sending more and more families below the poverty line.

They were joined by large numbers of small farmers but not by the upper crust of large landowners. By 1975 the top 10 per cent of the rural population were enjoying substantially higher real incomes, boosted by the rising price of rice, which they alone could afford to sell, and by the accumulation of more land, which they alone could afford to buy.

Table 2. Landlessness in rural Bangladesh

Year	Landless labourers as percentage of cultivators	Number of landless (millions)
1951	14.3	1.51
1961	17.5	2.47
1963-64	17.8	2.71
1967-68	19.8	3.40

Bangladesh suffers from poor resources and a high population density. These combine with a low growth in agricultural production to explain much of the concentration of rural poverty in Bangladesh today. But the increase and depth of that poverty has been made worse by the increasing level of inequality, particularly in landholding. The inability of small farmers to maintain their incomes in the face of rising inflation, the low level of job creation in rural areas–which attacks directly the earning power of agricultural labourers–and the increasing dependence on wage labour itself, all have their root cause in the high concentration of land among the relative few.

The consequence has been that the purchasing power of three-quarters of the rural population–the fifth largest in the world–has been obliterated. Over half live with an income that can supply only malnutrition. In contrast, the top 10 per cent of the population have been able to increase their real income and, with that income, increase the inequality in landholding that helps to perpetuate such levels of acute poverty.

TAMIL NADU:
THE GREEN REVOLUTION AND INCREASING POVERTY

The state of Tamil Nadu in south-east India is the seventh most populated state in India (1971, 41.2 million). On the face of it the state should be one of the most prosperous. Between 1950 and 1971 Tamil Nadu averaged an annual growth of 5.3 per cent in its total wealth. While mining and manufacturing doubled their share of the state's output, agriculture showed an over-all growth as well: food grains averaged a 4.5 per cent increase per annum throughout this period. With a growth in population of only 1.85 per cent a year, food production was well in line with the increase in population. With real income per head 51 per cent higher at the end of the second decade everyone should have been better off. They were not.

Two types of rural development

The agriculture of Tamil Nadu can be divided into three major sectors. The most important crop is rice, but it is grown on "wet" lands, which permit two crops a year and on "dry" lands, which allow only one. Needless to say, the former lands are by far the more prosperous. In addition, there are poorer millet farmers, located on the "dry" unirrigated lands. In both areas there is a smattering of cash crops, mainly groundnuts, sugar cane and cotton. Tea is grown on a few estates.

While the state's agriculture showed on over-all growth between 1951 and 1971 there were two distinct phases, broken in the mid-1960s by stagnation, drought and a decline in production.

Growth through irrigation

The first phase lasted from 1951 to 1962 and corresponded to the years of India's First and Second Five-Year Plans. These were the boom years of rice production: it increased by 83 per cent during this period. Other crops, with the exception of sugar cane, which expanded quickly, increased their production at a much more modest rate. Millets increased by only 20 per cent. Nevertheless, this decade saw the production of food grains rise from 3.6 million to 5.3 million tonnes.

The 1950s were the years of large-scale public investment in irrigation facilities. Thanks largely to the extensive development of government controlled canals and "tanks" the land under irrigation rose from 4.7 million to 6.2 million acres. This in turn permitted a tremendous increase in the area raising at least two crops a year. The double-cropped area jumped from 2.3 million acres to 3.26 million hectares.

Between 1962 and 1965 public investment in agriculture tailed off. The potential for extending large-scale public irrigation facilities was considered exhausted. This caused some confusion about how to develop next. During this period bad droughts hit the region and food production slumped.

The Green Revolution

In 1966-67 the Green Revolution was initiated. This programme offered a package of new high-yielding seed varieties combined with fertilisers, electricity, credit facilities and other extension services. But the new programme was deliberately selective, concentrating on the "efficient" farmers, who were considered to have both the motivation and facilities to take advantage of the new inputs.

Production certainly increased. The new seeds, watered by electrically driven "pump-sets" and well fertilised, raised rice production from 3.5 million tonnes in 1965-66 to 5.2 million tonnes by 1971-72, a 40 per cent increase in five years. It had been ten years since similar increases had taken place. But millet production actually declined, from 1.245 to 1.052 million tonnes. As the staple food of the poorer groups in rural areas this had an adverse effect on the weaker section of society.

Special programmes of assistance to small farmers were available but the benefits of growth were still highly selective. Everywhere the nature of the new programme and its distribution were such that, only those with a reasonable command of resources could respond effectively to the new schemes. Much of the increased rice production was dependent on possession of the new private irrigation facilities being offered–the pump-sets. By 1971, 470,000 were being used, but mainly by the larger and richer farmers. While the privately irrigated land rose from 1.73 to 1.98 million acres by 1971, publicly irrigated land fell from 4.7 to 4.35 million acres. The losers were the poorer farmers who could not afford to install the new pump-sets and those whose farm plots were too small to make viable use of the new investment.

Pattern of poverty

Despite its resources, poverty has always been widespread in Tamil Nadu. But the two distinct phases of growth in agriculture had markedly different effects on poverty. During the first phase the extent of poverty declined, but with the new strategy of selective growth the proportion of the rural population living below the poverty line took a dramatic upward turn, back to the level of the early 1950s.

Table 3 shows the extent of poverty at three points in time. Two indicators of poverty have been used. The first relates purely to food. This is the estimated cost of providing an average-sized rural family with a nutritionally adequate diet of 2,400 calories a day. In 1957-58, 53 per cent of the rural population did not earn sufficient to supply such a diet. By 1961-62, at the end of the first period of growth, this declined to 36 per cent. Then, while the Green Revolution increased food production to nearly 7 million tonnes a year, the proportion of the rural population earning less than enough to feed their families adequately increased again to over 48 per cent.

The second poverty line takes in more than food. This refers to the minimum income commonly considered necessary to provide an average rural family with all their basic needs: housing, clothing and state-provided health and education facilities. Again, during the first period of growth, the proportion of the rural population below this poverty line declined, from 74 per cent in 1957-58 to just over 66 per cent in 1961-62. Thereafter it rose, until by 1970 it was virtually at the level it had been in 1957–nearly three-quarters of the rural population without an income sufficient to fulfil basic needs.

Growth and inequality

During the past 20 years Tamil Nadu has experienced two periods of growth. In the 1950s government investment vastly increased the extent of public irrigation facilities. The decade saw a tremendous increase in food production, real incomes rose, as did real per head consumption. While chronic inequality in landholding continued to ensure that there was al-

Profiles of rural poverty

Table 3. Poverty in rural areas of Tamil Nadu

Year	Food line		Basic-needs line	
	Cost per month (Rupees)	Percentage of population earning less	Cost per month (Rupees)	Percentage of population earning less
1957-58	13.37	53.10	18.5	74.10
1961-62	15.90	36.04	22.00	66.49
1969-70	27.93	48.63	38.58	73.98

ways a large body of agricultural labourers who managed less well than others, there was a steady decline in the extent of rural poverty.

The second phase of growth was characterised by the selective application of the Green Revolution. Again food production rose sharply, but only for rice (plus some cash crops). New production facilities were "privatised", excluding many poorer farmers and were disproportionately utilised by larger farmers.

During this period all indicators of poverty–per head consumption, diet and basic-needs poverty lines–registered an alarming growth in its extent. The poverty was not just borderline: there was a bulging of poverty in the intermediate group of those in acute poverty.

With this growth in poverty came increasing inequality. Throughout this period more than 60 per cent of rural households owned less than 1 acre of land. Most could not take advantage of the new schemes, while others, like the "dry" millet farmer, were ignored–they were "marginalised". Over-all 56 per cent of all operational holdings in 1971 yielded an income barely sufficient to provide even a minimum level of living for cultivator families.

A similar fate faced many village artisans, as modernised production made redundant their traditional crafts–rice milling, jewellery and spinning. Over 85 per cent of artisan families were probably below the poverty line by the early 1970s.

With nearly 60 per cent of the land owned by the top 10 per cent of households the main impact of poverty was inevitably among labouring families; their numbers expanded by increasing landlessness and the decline of rural industries. In 1961, 51 per cent of agricultural workers were cultivators and 22 per cent agricultural labourers. By 1971 the figures were 40 and 38 per cent respectively. Urban employment failed to grow and the new agricultural strategy did not significantly expand the employment created in the late 1950s. More people looking for wage employment meant that the number of days worked, on average, by agricultural labourers continued to decline. With the real wage rate fluctuating wildly, 87 per cent of agricultural labouring families were receiving an income in 1971 insufficient to supply their basic needs.

Mass poverty exists because the mass of the people do not have, and under certain kinds of institutional patterns cannot contribute to, productive activity. It is a reflection of the total malfunctioning of the economic order, closely related to production processes, the manner in which resources are owned and utilised and to policy measures. In Tamil Nadu during the past ten years the choice of products and of techniques has been dictated by the wants of a few rather than the needs of the many. The system, therefore, cannot provide for the elementary needs of those who have no resources at their command with which to influence its working in their favour. The consequence is their increasing impoverishment.

MALAYSIA: GROWTH WITH INEQUALITY

Malaysia is exceptional in south Asia. The country is rich in natural resources–timber, tin, rubber, even new land is available–and relatively prosperous. Since independence, in 1957, its national income has grown at around 5 per cent a year. Though population growth was relatively high, at around 3 per cent per annum, by 1973 Malaysians enjoyed, at US$570 a head, the third highest per head income in the region.

Malaysia's resources reach into the rural areas. As well as rice, rubber is grown extensively both on estates, which account for about 20 per cent of agricultural employment, and on smallholdings which are usually less than 10 acres. However, at the time of independence rural poverty was widespread. The Government, whose power base had largely been the peasant agricultural sector, undertook an extensive rural development programme. By the early 1960s 25 per cent of all public investment was on rural development.

Selecting growth

Reflecting the dual nature of Malaysia's rural economy the Government focused its development schemes on rice and rubber. In both the emphasis was on increasing output. For rice this was to be achieved by more extensive irrigation facilities and by the provision of high-yielding varieties. By 1970 the area that was double-cropped had risen from a mere 1 per cent of paddy land to almost one-third, while high-yielding varieties had been introduced on half the paddy acreage. The effect of the programme was a tremendous increase in the productivity of every worker. In the ten years after independence output per worker rose by over 60 per cent.

In the rubber sector the Government concentrated on the smallholders. The estates represented powerful private and often foreign interests. Many owners were breaking up their estates, throwing their mainly Indian workers into unemployment–about one-fifth of estate workers lost their jobs. But for those remaining the National Union of Plantation Workers was a powerful and effective arbitrator. Despite declining rubber prices the wages of estate workers rose steadily between 1957 and 1970. Wages increased by almost 40 per cent, significantly higher than the 23 per cent increase in the value of output per worker; employment, however, fell by 18 per cent.

For smallholders the Government followed a two-tier scheme. One was the introduction of high-yielding clones. At the same time virgin land was turned into 10-acre rubber farms. By 1970, 500,000 acres of new land had been brought into cultivation, high-yielding varieties accounted for 60 per cent smallholding acreage (it was 12 per cent in 1957) and productivity per worker had risen by 26 per cent.

The combination of more intensive production with extending acreage brought a substantial growth in the output of both rice and rubber. With it should have come increasing prosperity and declining inequality. Neither occurred.

Increasing inequality

Table 4 shows that, over-all, the Government's schemes succeeded– just. The average monthly income in rural Malaysia rose in real terms. (i.e. taking account of inflation), though only by 7 per cent. But for the poorest 60 per cent of the rural population the programme failed; their real incomes declined and it was worse for the very poor. Between 1957 and 1970 the monthly real income of the poorest 20 per cent of rural Malaysia fell from 55.8 Malaysian dollars to 32.7. This 40 per cent fall in living standards for the poorest group was not experienced by the richest–their incomes rose by more than 20 per cent during this period, to average 471.6 Malaysian dollars. As a result, the inequality between the poorest and richest groups in rural Malaysia doubled; from a ratio of 7:1 in 1957 to 14:1 in 1970. This occurred precisely at a time when rural development was the main plank of the Government's programme. Why is this?

One factor is external to the Malaysian economy. Between 1957 and 1970 world rubber prices declined sharply–by 40 per cent–and the effect was obviously felt by rubber smallholders. But those with low-yielding varieties and those with the new higher-yielding trees suffered a 60 per cent fall in net income per acre.

While this is an important element in the Malaysian experience, it is not sufficient to explain either the across-the-board decline in rural incomes for all the poorest–whether they grow rubber or not–or why the poorest should suffer exclusively.

Limiting growth

For a start, the poorest rubber smallholders fared worst. While farms with both high- and low-yielding varieties suffered a similar decline in the

Profiles of poverty

Table 4. Distribution of income in rural Malaysia, 1957 and 1970 (Malaysian dollars per month)

Income groups (%)	1957	1970
0-20	55.8	32.7
20-40	97.4	81.8
40-60	132.2	130.2
60-80	189.1	201.7
80-100	388.6	471.6
Over-all	172.6	184.5

price for their rubber, the net income per acre for those with low-yielding trees was virtually half that of those with high-yielding trees. The consequence of declining rubber prices was, therefore, far worse for the poorer group of farmers.

The poorest farmers, with the smallest plots, could not afford to replant with the new varieties, despite the subsidised replanting scheme. It takes around seven years for a rubber tree to become fully productive; this gestation period is being shortened, but during the 1960s this fact was crucial. While larger holdings could replant in stages, leaving fully productive trees to maintain income, very small holdings and those near the subsistence level could not do this. Unfortunately, there was no special loan scheme to meet this problem. Farmers suffering this fate probably accounted for 35 per cent of those employed in the rubber smallholding sector.

Over-all, less than 25 per cent of smallholders experienced an increase in their real incomes in this period and most of them were the favoured few who were settled on government land-development schemes. Between 1957 and 1970, 40,700 rural households benefited from this scheme–a mere 4.7 per cent of 1957 rural households.

The selectiveness of these development schemes applies to paddy farmers also, as much of the new investment in rice was restricted to the already prosperous regions of Malaysia. Almost half the paddy land did not benefit from either irrigation or high-yielding varieties. Significantly, the poorest paddy growing areas of Kelantan and Malacca benefited least. In Kelantan, the second-most important rice growing state and the one with the greatest concentration of population, there was actually a decrease in acreage. Only 61,000 families benefited from double-cropping facilities between 1957 and 1970.

Other factors contributed to worsening the lot of the poorest groups. In Kelantan, for example, output per acre declined while average rental levels rose by more than 80 per cent. With the guaranteed minimum price for rice falling by 4 per cent in real terms and population growth pressurising land into smaller holdings, the farm incomes of the poorest groups were squeezed from all sides. In all, by 1970, only 11 per cent of the 1957 popu-

Profiles of rural poverty

lation had benefited from the Government's extensive rural development drive.

Once again the lack of non-farm employment further constrained income-earning opportunities. The rice schemes tended to merely take up the slack of under-utilised labour by farm families, leaving nothing for hired labour. Rural unemployment levels rose and between 1962 and 1967 the number of people claiming to work less than 25 hours a week rose from 146,800 to 267,300–an 80 per cent increase in only five years. Despite heavy investment and increased production the old problem of underemployment and hence low incomes still remains in rural Malaysia.

Conclusion

Malaysia's development strategy since independence has been a rural-oriented one, but its concern with growth only has meant that it paid little attention to the needs of the poorest sections of the population.

Within a general belief that Malaysia had abundant untapped resources, especially of arable land, there has been a deliberate attempt to create a privileged "prosperous peasantry". New settlers were often selected from the landless, but they were given 10 acres of land when 97 per cent of rice farms and 76 per cent of rubber smallholdings were well below this level. Given population growth and the extent of land available, a 10-acre ceiling is totally unrealistic as a long-term solution to rural poverty.

The strategy has tried to intensify the production of the few, particularly in rice. From this, it was hoped, spill-over effects would benefit other, poorer, sections of the rural comunity. The actual effect has been to localise growth and to restrict it to those capable of taking advantage of it. In this way, public investment has focused on the wrong groups and has not been sufficiently general.

The actual pattern of rural development created a queue for higher income-earning opportunities. The bottlenecks in this queue, which ensured it moved slowly, adversely affected the weakest section of the peasantry who either did not receive, or could not respond to, the new opportunities for raising incomes.

The solution to this problem does not lie in a piecemeal removal of these bottlenecks. The queue might then move a bit faster, but there is a finite level to the incomes it can generate and it does nothing to solve the problem of increasing inequality. To reduce this, new policies would have to be more precisely aimed at the needs of the poorer sectors of the rural population and more generally fundamental in their impact. Land reform, the manipulation of relative prices, the provision of extension services to poorer "marginal farmers" have not been contemplated or pushed with significant vigour to do this. They will need to be if inequality and poverty are to be reduced.

Profiles of poverty

CHINA:
EGALITARIAN DEVELOPMENT

The history of China in the past 30 years has been a source of fascination for many of those interested in rural development; a fascination that has had to survive on very little hard evidence. China, with its vast area, huge and diverse resources and particular political development may appear, on first view, to have little of relevance to the problems examined in this book. Yet, despite its resources, in the 1920s and 1930s its society was typical of many developing countries today—agricultural, poor and unequal. In 1957 about 86 per cent of the Chinese people still lived in rural areas and yet, from all accounts, its society has been transformed, poverty all but removed and agricultural production keeping steadily ahead of the growth in population.

The path the Chinese have taken to bring this transformation about is only one possible way to reduce poverty, but it contains many of the features necessary to any attempt to secure the basic needs of all the people. At the same time, the examination of continuing inequality in China pinpoints the dangers and problems that are likely to confront any attempt to establish a more equal society.

First step forward

Pre-Revolutionary China was a land of inequalities, as table 5 demonstrates. Small farmers, who represented 23 per cent of all farm families, owned less than 6 per cent of all land, whilst the top 4 per cent of landowners owned nearly 30 per cent. Many of the small farmers, possessing on average only 1.4 acres, rented more land from landlords at an exhorbitant rent. Over half of all rural families were in debt. It has been calculated that, allowing for debt repayment, the vast majority of small and medium farmers produced less than 80 per cent of their families' subsistence requirement. Below these were a significant number of landless labourers in an even worse plight.

Making rough calculations it is plausible to argue that at the most the income share of the bottom 20 per cent of the rural population was between 5 and 6 per cent, while that of the top 20 per cent was at least 45 per cent. The degree of inequality in rural China in the 1920s was not very different from what it is in an average country in south and south-east Asia today.

Between 1949 and 1952 a highly egalitarian land reform took place. The poor peasants and the landless were organised at the grassroots by the political movement that carried out the Revolution and the peasants themselves were encouraged to take the land by overthrowing their local oppressors.

Land reforms brought about a massive redistribution of income and wealth in favour of the poor peasants and at the cost of the landlords. The reforms were not "class neutral", involving merely the imposition of a

Profiles of rural poverty

Table 5. Distribution of land in pre-Revolution China

Category	Percentage of all farm households	Average size of farm (acres)	Percentage share of all owned land
Small farmers	23.1	1.43	5.8
Medium farmers	35.6	2.84	17.7
Medium-large farmers	19.2	4.92	16.6
Large farmers	10.6	7.17	13.6
Very large farmers	7.7	12.66	17.6
Landlords	3.8	.	28.7

hypothetical ceiling on land owned. Land was appropriated by the peasants and the "rentiers" in particular were subjected to a much greater degree of expropriation than other landowners.

The categories in table 6 do not correspond to the previous categories. Poor peasants in the table now include those that were previously landless, which is why they now account for over half of all rural families. The tremendous significance of the Chinese land reforms lies in the fact that this new group now possesses nearly half the land, with an average farm size of 2 acres. The shares of landlords and rich peasants have all but been obliterated. The result is a massive reduction in inequality. From an average ratio of 8:1 the inequality between top and bottom income groups was reduced to less than 3:1. Yet the new society of landed peasantry maintained the efficiency of production.

Seventeen per cent of the national income that had previously gone into rents and profits and from there into the conspicuous consumption of the rich was redistributed to the poor and middle peasants. Much of it found its way to savings in the form of self-financed investment and increased payments to the State, in the form of both direct and concealed taxes. By 1952 about 35 per cent of China's gross investments were being financed by savings generated as a direct consequence of the land reforms.

But while the society was more equal it still did not necessarily offer the same opportunities to all. Middle peasants in particular did very well out of the land-reform programmes. They strove to increase their wealth by renting in land, which was still permitted, while continuing debts forced others to sell or rent out their land. In this situation a gradual repolarisation of land ownership could be seen to be emerging.

The Great Leap Forward

The next stage of the Chinese agrarian revolution was the gradual collectivisation of the land. Table 7 charts this course starting with the mutual aid teams, where individual farms voluntarily pooled their labour and tools. Many of these were then merged into elementary co-operatives, where common property was more widespread but land was still owned privately and families received dividends on their land shares and certain payments for the pooling of their farm tools and draught animals.

Table 6. Distribution of land after the land reforms

Category	Percentage of rural households	Average area owned (acres)	Percentage share of owned land
Poor peasant	57.1	2.00	46.8
Middle peasant	35.8	3.05	44.8
Rich peasant	3.6	4.33	6.4
Landlord	2.6	1.97	2.1
Others	0.9	.	.

Then in 1956 came the drive to organise peasant families into more socialist and larger advanced co-operatives, where land and other means of production ceased to be privately owned and the total output of the land was distributed solely on the basis of the work put in by individual families.

Yet income inequalities continued to exist. In particular, the middle peasants continued to have a much higher average income than that of the rural population as a whole. Between 1956 and 1957 evidence suggests that middle peasants enhanced their privileged position, while the per head incomes of poor peasants declined.

Finally, in 1958, the transformation of the advanced co-operatives into the people's communes took place during the Great Leap Forward. The larger-sized communes became the sole owners of all land and productive assets and also became the accounting unit for the income distribution.

Present system

The commune structure remains the basis for Chinese agriculture today. Communes can average over 30,000 people. Below them are the production brigades of some 1,500 to 3,000 people and below these the production teams of a hundred or so people. Since 1958 the roles of each tier and its importance in controlling the distribution of income has fluctuated as the Chinese people wrestle with the problem of persistent inequality on the one hand and the need to maximise food production on the other.

The gains by the middle peasantry in the early co-operatives can be explained by the tendency to distribute income solely on the basis of work points. Long experience of independent farm management gave them greater skills to earn work points than those who had once been agricultural labourers. In the early communes the criterion of need was assigned a very considerable weight and virtually a fixed-wage system was introduced. In addition, income was determined by the average productivity of a number of co-operatives of varying degrees of prosperity.

At the time, this system led to resentments and a tendency to reduce the incentive to work. In 1961 the team was made the basic accounting unit and the principle of work capacity was restored. Usually, however, the daily wage rate for the ablest and most skilled worker is only a third higher than that of the least able and skilled–though, for uncertain reasons, the wage rate for women is lower than that of men.

Profiles of rural poverty

Table 7. Socialist transformation of Chinese agriculture, 1952 to 1958 (Percentage of peasant families)

Year	Individual farms	Mutual aid teams	Elementary co-operatives	Advanced co-operatives	People's communes
1952	60.0	39.9	0.1	–	–
1953	60.5	39.3	0.2	–	–
1954	39.7	58.3	2.0	–	–
1955	35.1	50.7	14.2	–	–
1956	3.7	–	8.5	87.8	–
1957	2.0	–	2.0	96.0	–
1958	.	–	.	.	99.1

As all workers gained more experience income based on work capacity was no longer such a source of inequality. However, many communes combine this system with an automatic distribution of the basic food needs of the family. As this combined system has developed and proved acceptable, attempts have been made to grapple with the differences between teams–in their land, dependency ratio, etc. As a result, in many communes the larger brigades are becoming the basic accounting unit for distributing income.

Though more remote from the individual family, the larger the basic accounting unit the smaller the degree of inequality is likely to be. Nevertheless, regional differences in land availability, soil fertility, etc., produce marked differences in per head income between communes; something like 4:1. The Government is attempting to deal with this problem: communes in poor areas are given preferential treatment, and credit facilities are made available to them and recruitment for urban jobs is often exclusively from the poorer regions.

Despite many continuing problems the effect of the Chinese way to rural development has been impressive. Class origin has ceased to be a major source of income inequality. Though regional differences, demographic factors and the resource endowment of individual teams continue to be important sources of differences, Chinese society is now significantly more equal. In addition, the Government has done much to ensure it is less poor. All communes strive for the goal of self-sufficiency. Although many do not achieve it, food, unlike in other Asian countries, is cheap relative to the price of other products such as clothes or bicycles. This is supplemented by an egalitarian distribution of health, housing and educational facilities.

In 1966, in a study of 18 communes, the lowest wage recorded for a family was 100 yuan; or 50 yuan per person in an average family, given that an equivalent of 20 yuan was probably earned from the private plot.

With an average daily calorie requirement of 2,100 per person, the basic food cost per person would be 34.8 yuan. The cost of clothing (cotton) is roughly 5.70 yuan. Housing is provided; so are schools, health facilities and welfare payments for extra dependants. This means 20 per cent of this low income is still free for the purchase of other basic needs. Even the poorest families in the poorest region can provide their basic food needs, receive communal services and still have 20 per cent of their income to spend on other basic needs.

Although precise calculations cannot be made it is safe to say that, today, the poorest 20 per cent of China's population earn over 11 per cent of national income, while the top 20 per cent earn only 35 per cent. No other Asian country can match that and few can say that, while life may be very austere, poverty, in the sense of inadequate food, clothing and shelter, does not exist.

POVERTY AND LANDLESSNESS IN AFRICA AND LATIN AMERICA

3

1 Chad
2 Ivory Coast
3 Sudan
4 Tanzania
5 Zambia

6 Bolivia
7 Brazil
8 Colombia
9 Costa Rica
10 Peru

Profiles of rural poverty

Evidence on Africa and Latin America is far less satisfactory than that on Asia.[1] Whatever data are available should be interpreted with great caution especially when inter-country comparisons are contemplated. Nevertheless, existing evidence for these two continents, fragmentary as it may be, suggests that the experience of worsening poverty despite rapid economic growth may not be unique to Asia.

To start with Latin America, the distribution of incomes in rural areas shows a high degree of inequality (see table 8); higher, perhaps, than in some Asian countries. Information on hand is scarce, but in at least one Latin American country–Brazil, which has the largest concentration of rural population in the whole region–there appears to have been a substantial increase in inequality: the Gini coefficient for income distribution in rural Brazil rose from 0.4743 in 1960 to 0.5780 in 1970. These figures on inequality imply the existence of a large problem of poverty. In table 9 we put together some estimates of the rural population in poverty in some Latin American countries. The picture is one of widespread misery. Out of 155.6 million rural population in Latin America 90.8 million, or 58 per cent, live below the poverty line, i.e. find it difficult to gain an income which satisfies their basic human needs. Certainly, this average hides important inter-country variations. For instance, while the rural poor represent only 8 per cent of the rural population in Argentina their ratio goes up to 53 per cent in Mexico, 67 per cent in Brazil and as high as 80 per cent in Honduras. These percentages tell the story of over 90 million people who live in poverty.

Data on Africa are even less abundant than on Latin America but whatever is available points to similar conclusions. Table 10 sums up some measures of inequality in the distribution of rural incomes in some African countries. With the exception of Botswana there appears to be a certain degree of equality in the distribution of rural incomes. But income estimates in rural Africa are often of doubtful reliability. Moreover, equality so far as it exists really in many sub-Saharan countries would in fact mean equality at very low levels of income. This is reflected in the high degree of incidence of poverty in many African countries. According to some recent estimates the proportion of households in poverty amounted to 51 per cent in northern Nigeria, 70 per cent in Sierra Leone, 74 per cent in Ghana, 88 per cent in both Kenya and Tanzania, and was as high as 91 per cent in Lesotho.[2] If these figures are correct, the extent of rural poverty is really tremendous in the African context.

One important factor in explaining inequality and widespread poverty in Africa as well as in Latin America is the unequal distribution of productive assets, notably land. Table 11 shows that for Latin America the degree of concentration in the distribution of land ownership is not only high but in some cases increasing. In Africa, with the exception of some countries (Zaire, Zambia and Botswana), the degree of concentration may be less than in Latin America, but it must be remembered that in a land-abundant continent it is not only land that accounts for differentiation among the peasantry but also the ownership of other assets such as livestock, the control of water and the degree of benefit from government expenditure.

Table 8. Relative inequality: Gini coefficients of income distribution in Latin America

Country	Year	Rural
Argentina	1961	0.5311
Brazil	1960	0.4743
	1970	0.5780
Chile	1968	0.4280
Colombia	1960	0.5922
	1970	0.4764
Costa Rica	1961	0.5310
	1971	0.3674
Ecuador	1965	0.6783
El Salvador	1961	0.5242
Guatemala	1966	0.2996
Honduras	1967/68	0.4861
Mexico	1963	0.5309
Puerto Rico	1963	0.4236
Venezuela	1963	0.4607

Source: Based on Shail Jain: *Size distribution of income: A compilation of data* (IBRD, Washington, 1975).

Table 9. Latin America: rural population in poverty, 1970

Country	Total rural population (000's) (1)	Rural population in poverty[1] (000's) (2)	(2) ÷ (1) % (3)
Argentina	7 885	631	8
Brazil	56 338	37 746	67
Colombia	11 332	5 666	50
Costa Rica	1 367	451	33
Chile	3 502	1 331	38
Honduras	2 118	1 694	80
Mexico	31 255	16 565	53
Peru	8 095	5 100	63
Uruguay	976	127	13
Venezuela	4 358	1 395	32
Others	28 441	20 045	70
Total	155 667	90 751	58

[1] Those population whose incomes were not sufficient to satisfy their basic needs.
Source: Based on data from ILO (PREALC): *Empleo, distribución del ingreso y necesidades básicas en América latina* (Santiago, June 1978), Table 1-1, p. 1-3.

Table 10. Rural Africa: some estimates of inequality in rural areas

Country	Year	Gini coefficients, rural incomes
Botswana	1974/75	0.52
Lesotho	1970/71	0.35
Sierra Leone	1974/75	0.32
Zambia	1972/73	0.39
Sudan	1967/68	0.35

Source: Quoted from ILO: *Poverty and employment in rural areas of developing countries*, Report II, Advisory Committee on Rural Development, Ninth Session, Geneva, 1979.

Table 11. Gini coefficients of concentration in the distribution of landholding in selected countries, 1960 and 1970

Country	1960	1970
Africa		
Algeria	.	0.6575[1]
Botswana	.	0.5011
Cameroon (United Rep. of)	.	0.4446
Central African Empire	.	0.3713
Chad	.	0.3700
Congo	.	0.2893
Gabon	.	0.4745
Ivory Coast	.	0.4229
Lesotho	.	0.3827
Malawi	.	0.3634
Sierra Leone	.	0.4382
Zaire	.	0.8848
Zambia	.	0.7566
Latin America		
Costa Rica	0.7816	0.8164
Dominican Republic	0.8040	0.7942
Panama	0.7352	0.7842
Puerto Rico	0.7383	0.7867
Uruguay	0.8267	0.8238
Brazil	.	0.8379
Peru	.	0.7758
Jamaica	.	0.7930

[1] Refers to private land ownership and does not include land in the "socialist sector".

Sources: ILO: *Poverty and employment in rural areas of developing countries*, op. cit. Gini coefficients for distribution of landholdings based on data from the 1960 and 1970 Census of Agriculture in the respective countries as reported in FAO: *Report on the 1970 World Census of Agriculture, Country Bulletins*, Rome, 1975; and Asian Development Bank: *Rural Asia: challenge and opportunity* (Praeger, New York, 1978) Table I.5.8.

Notes

[1] Research is under way on dimensions and causes of rural poverty in Africa and Latin America.

[2] ILO: *Poverty and employment in the rural areas of developing countries*, Report II, Advisory Committee on Rural Development, Ninth Session, Geneva, 1979.

CONCLUDING REMARKS

LESSONS AND EXPERIENCE

Now we come to the end of our survey. The "Asian Drama" is still with us. Despite the rise in average incomes over the past two decades, the incidence of rural poverty has shown little tendency to diminish and, in many cases, the standard of living of some socio-economic groups, notably the landless, has actually declined. The reasons for this, it has also been suggested, have less to do with aggregate or sectoral rates of growth than with such factors as the distribution of productive assets, the pattern of government investment and the non-neutrality of technological advance. As regards other continents, the above pieces of evidence, fragmentary as they may be, leave us with the unmistakable impression that the experience of growth in the last quarter of a century has not succeeded in mitigating the problem of rural poverty in Africa and Latin America.

THE CHALLENGE TO THE THIRD WORLD

What is to be done?
The community of Third World countries is certainly aware of the extent and nature of the problem of poverty in general and rural poverty in particular. Many policies and programmes have been devised to make the assault on poverty but, unfortunately, the results fell far short of hopes. One reason may have been that these programmes did not go far enough, another is that they addressed the wrong questions or in some cases did not go beyond the planning stage. Policy options for poverty eradication are certainly not beyond the imagination of planners and policy-makers in the Third World. Probably what is needed is the will to face up to the challenge of the obscenity of modern times: poverty.

APPENDIX: NOTE ON CHART 5

Essentially, poverty is a *relative* concept; people are poor if they cannot afford those things in life that the society in which they live regards as a normal part of their standard of living. In many rich countries families who cannot afford a car are often considered "poor". But in the developing world the prevalence of destitution, hunger and disease enables an additional *absolute* concept of poverty to be used.

The concept of a *poverty line* is an attempt to set a *minimum* standard of living, in terms of diet, clothing, sanitation; one that permits a family to lead a relatively healthy and active life, even if they are deprived in other areas such as work and schooling. The poverty line is not an acceptable standard of living, but it is an attempt to distinguish between health and hunger.

Poverty lines are usually based on the income calculated to be necessary to keep an average family at this minimum standard of living. This leads to two sets of problems. One is finding the correct income equivalent in a situation where wages are often paid in kind, or families supplement their food supply by home-grown produce, or by scavenging. The second problem is that the *minimum* standard of living varies from region to region and from occupation to occupation. In particular this relates to the required food intake for a healthy life–and its cost. Official United Nations requirements, for example, calculate that 2,100 calories per person per day are needed in Pakistan; in Bangladesh the figure is 2,150. But workers performing heavy labour need much more than this. In Bangladesh it has been calculated that an average labourer requires 3,880 calories a day because of the heavy labour involved.

Poverty lines can rarely be this sensitive. At best they are a rough-and-ready guide to the order of magnitude of poverty. Differences in the basis for calculating the poverty lines in the ILO studies means that the levels reported in chart 5 are not comparable. For Bangladesh and Pakistan the poverty line equals an income estimated sufficient to supply 90 per cent of the official calorie requirement for each region. The Indian case studies are based on the official monthly income calculated as being sufficient to provide the minimum basic needs–not just food. Malaysia and the Philippines are again based on differing income calculations and refer to the percentage of rural *households* living in poverty, not the population. Similar calculations were not available for Sri Lanka and Indonesia, but other evidence, quoted in the text, strongly suggests that the same would apply. Poverty, however measured but always less than the barest minimum, covers a significant and often increasing proportion of rural people.

Furthermore, it must be stressed that the levels of poverty shown in chart 5 are inevitably an underestimate. In some cases the poverty line used is less than the

Profiles of rural poverty

official minimum, in all a generous allowance for home-grown or gathered produce has been made. Again, the calorie levels are the average intake needed, they make no allowance for the extra energy needed by those performing heavy labour–and inevitably the poor are always those engaged in heavy manual work. Finally, the concept of the poverty line does not indicate how far below the minimum many families are living. Evidence in the profiles on Bangladesh and Tamil Nadu shows that many families are living on an income far below that considered to be the minimum. In many ways the estimates of poverty given in chart 5 are a conservative estimate of the number of people now living in poverty.

HC
415
.P6
P76

5549